Papier Mâché

Peter Rush
Papier Mâché

Farrar Straus Giroux • New York

First published in the United States
of America in 1980 by
Farrar, Straus and Giroux, Inc.
Copyright © Peter Rush 1980
Colour photographs copyright © Victor Albrow 1980

Library of Congress Cataloging in Publication Data
Rush, Peter. Papier mâché.
    Includes index.
    1. Papier-mâché. I. Title.
TT871.R88 1980   745.54'2   80–18097

Colour photographs by Victor Albrow.
Photographs on pages 1 and 85 by
Pat Keene; photograph on page 93 by
Irene Barry.
All drawings by the author.

Contents

Introduction

About fourteen years ago, a young designer came to see me at the magazine offices. Unlike most, he wasn't accompanied by the usual large black portfolio, but carried an immaculate custom-built case.

It was opened to reveal a set of the most perfect papier mâché figures that I had seen, for they went far beyond my preconceived ideas of this particular art form. This was my introduction to Peter Rush's work.

Over the years Peter has provided a marvellous range of models. Commissions have ranged from a full-size Jersey cow to a series of portrait characters of famous people in prehistoric guise!

This delightful book tells us how it can be achieved. The only thing missing is the one secret ingredient, the touch of magic that only Peter Rush possesses.

Geof Axby
art director *Sunday Telegraph Magazine*

for Jane and for Stephanie

I would like to thank Suzi Siddons for her generous help and vigorous editing

Foreword

I would like to explain how the approach here to modelling in paper differs from that in other books on the subject.

Firstly, since 1900 the most outstanding influence on the development of papier mâché has been the consistent use of newspaper as its basic material and this has really determined what can be attempted.

Newspaper is considered here as only one of the long list of possible papers and materials open to us. Each kind of paper is seen to have its own characteristics and is usually good for modelling just one or two things. So, if we are cunning, we choose exactly the right paper to achieve our end with the minimum of fuss. All we need to know of any paper is: what kind of folds and creases will it make?

Medium-thick brown paper, for example, simulates canvas or raincoat material. Thick brown paper for leather. Tissue paper is excellent for lace and cotton: pulled taut it imitates satin. Typing paper is ideal for shirts and heavy skirts: doubled up it works well for suits and military clothing. Paper handkerchiefs are very good for picking up the

9

characteristics of loose skin and so on. Newspaper, in fact, being very stiff and springy, is rarely used.

Introduced to papier mâché as a schoolchild, the initial spark of interest was dampened down for twenty years under this soggy grey newspaper mash, and I'm afraid that lumpy looking ashtrays and nut bowls did little to revive it. Perhaps I was unlucky; nevertheless, it still happens to children today.

When we use tissue paper softened with cellulose wall-paper paste, we are using the very same organic materials that we are trying to simulate, ie tissue and cells. In the making of a head, for example, the tissue paper is packed hard and tight for bone (forehead, cheekbones and bridge of the nose); made into small rolls and pulled taut we have the muscles. Small pieces of tissue paper laid over these muscles become skin, and pulled out into fine fibrous shreds we have hair. The effect of all this can be startlingly realistic.

When the model is completed and dry before painting, it is given a coat of white emulsion. This not only conveniently fills up the cracks and helps to unite the model, but all the different types of paper and materials that have been used become neutralized under this fresh white skin. Part of the interest is then that anyone looking at the model is at a loss to know either how it was made or from what material.

The development of
papier mâché

By the end of the second century AD the Chinese had invented paper, made then from mulberry bark, cotton, vegetable fibre and linen rags. Paper making was slow, laborious work and therefore expensive, so it would follow that good use was put to off-cuts and scrap. Two papier mâché helmets, toughened by being lacquered, survive from this period and these are the first examples of papier mâché that we know of. It is interesting to us, who, over the last fifty years or so, have come to think of papier mâché as an essentially transitory medium, that it should have ever been used for something so serious as armour, and also that a specimen should survive for nearly two thousand years.

From China, paper making spread to Japan and to Persia where it was used largely for making masks and festival ornaments. By AD 900 the technique of moulding paper, stiffened and waterproofed with copal varnish, was known in Europe, and by the seventeenth century this technique was being used extensively for small, useful and decorative objects; papier mâché manufacture grew rapidly in confidence and dexterity through the eighteenth and nineteenth centuries, culminating in the ornate and elaborately decorated furnishings that we see in museums.

Towards the end of the seventeenth century we know of a manufacturer called Wilton of Charing Cross, London, who was producing architectural mouldings, cornices, scrolls, rosettes, wall brackets and decorative ornaments for attaching to chimney pieces, and furniture made from papier mâché; these weighing only a fraction of their plaster and stucco counterparts. It was through her trade with the Orient that England was attracted to the decorative side of papier mâché and set about first imitating and then developing the exotic oriental lacquered furniture that was to blossom and flourish in the Georgian and Victorian periods.

The simplest example of papier mâché that you could find would be a schoolboy's 'spitball': a small wad of exercise-book paper lovingly chewed and moulded into a deadly missile for his catapult; papier mâché means 'mashed or chewed paper' and it may be that the French émigré workers (from whom we get the word), working in the papier mâché shops in London during the eighteenth century, really did prepare the paper by chewing it for moulding small objects. Certainly, manufacturers did nothing to discourage the popularity of this idea, as it helped to shroud in mystery exactly how they did prepare their papier mâché. So jealously guarded were their methods of preparation that even today we know only that papier mâché was made with a binder of glue or gum arabic, flour, sawdust, resin, wax and plaster, or combinations of these with probably other ingredients that we know nothing of.

A manufacturer named John Baskerville, known for his fine books and typefounding, in about 1740 began successfully imitating the lacquered papier mâché pieces from Japan and subsequently this lacquering technique was known as 'japanning'. His assistant, Henry Clay, invented a method of preparing papier mâché that was not only stronger than wood but virtually heat-proof. Paper pulp was mixed with glue or gum arabic and the pulp stream kneaded and passed through rollers to achieve a slab of uniform thickness. This was dried slowly at a low temperature to prevent warping. The panels that he moulded from papier mâché were made up of ten or more sheets of soft, unsized paper, both sides of each sheet pasted with a mixture of boiled glue and flour and laid into a mould; this was drenched in linseed oil and dried at a temperature of 38°C (100°F). They were then ready to be used as panels for ceilings and partitions. They were extremely popular for all types of wheeled carriages, being light, strong and resilient.

When Henry Clay's patent expired many small firms sprang up, centred mainly in Birmingham and Wolverhampton, and the production of virtually everything from buttons to beds began in earnest. It is from these firms we get the beautiful, rich, black enamel papier mâché, gilded and decorated with flakes of mother of pearl. These flakes were softened, cut to shape and laid in position on the piece to be decorated; the thick, black varnish was built up in layers around it. This black varnish was a mixture of amber,

Writing case with mother-of-pearl inlay

Chair, circa 1850

linseed oil, resin and asphaltum thinned with turpentine: asphaltum was a bitumous substance coming from the Dead Sea and commonly known as 'Jewish glue'.

'Jenners and Bettridge' is the name we associate with this period: a Birmingham firm boasting shops in London and New York, it produced papier mâché objects of superb quality and decoration which are now largely museum pieces.

By 1860 the production of papier mâché reached a degree of perfection that precluded it from being used as a material for the new mass-production techniques; manufacturers were impatient to cater more speedily to a growing wealthier section of the population. They turned their attention to laminated wood, iron, plaster and plastic and, suddenly, papier mâché was out of fashion. A contributing factor to the rapid decline may have been that the new dresses of the day, with their starched and heavy underskirts, would simply send the lightweight chairs and small tables flying. Social mishaps like these would not have to occur very often before the offending pieces would be removed to the servants' rooms or nursery, never to return.

In any event, the great days of papier mâché were over, and japanners took their skills over to the new car and bicycle industries.

The Victoria Regina cot. Designed for Jenners and Betteridge, magnificently ugly, but a good example of papier mâché dexterity in its heyday

Papier mâché has had a rather more virile recent history in America. Perhaps there is something in the American temperament that is more in tune with the versatility of papier mâché, which is a very lively art/craft medium there today.

Papier mâché was first introduced to America by one William Allgood, a Northamptonshire Quaker and a leading expert in japanning. He started the highly successful Litchfield Manufacturing Company, remembered now for its richly decorated clock cases. Papier mâché survived not so much as a trade, as it had in England, but as a craft, taken up by women to provide themselves with all manner of useful and decorative household objects, developing their skills in papier mâché very much as they had done in their quilt work. The art of papier mâché was given a boost in the 1960s by a successful artist/designer, called Gemma, from New York, working with her husband in Mexico. Although her work there bore no relation to the traditional Mexican papier mâché which had long been used for making festival decorations, masks and traditional dolls, she attracted the interest of Mexican artists, who emulated and were later taught by her, with her beautiful applied papier mâché. From this a thriving industry has developed with a strong following in the United States.

15

Again in America, papier mâché is being applied to existing objects, mostly furniture, giving new life to things which would otherwise be discarded. This, coupled with the sophisticated use of modern materials, like automobile enamels for giving perfect and durable finishes, is a lovely instance of combining the best of the old with the best of the new.

In the heyday of papier mâché there were men like Isaac Weld, an Irishman from County Cork, who in 1800 made a boat from papier mâché and sailed it on the lakes of Killarney; and in 1833 Charles Frederick Bielefeld built ten prefabricated cottages and a ten-roomed villa for transportation to Australia at the request of a client for his party to inhabit instantly on arrival. This papier mâché village could be assembled in just four hours.

Charles Bielefeld's prefabricated papier mâché house, taken from a drawing which appeared in the Illustrated London News *in 1853. The rest of his houses were rather more utility. This must have been the absolute minimum that a Victorian gentleman of means considered tolerable living quarters. The inside was as handsomely appointed as the outside*

The disappointment that men like Weld and Bielefeld would feel if they were unlucky enough to come back and witness the dwindling away to near non-existence in England of this easy-going medium can only be guessed at; particularly in the face of the staggering production (not to say waste) of paper today. (It is a sobering thought that for one edition of a Sunday newspaper sixteen acres of forests are used.) All this and the tremendous range of acrylics, epoxies, polyurethanes, varnishes, lacquers, enamels and spray paints, the possibilities of which would have simply made them weak at the knees.

Perhaps a latter-day Charles Bielefeld will introduce papier mâché for building again, using our over-abundance of waste paper, possibly for building on known earth-tremor lines; the paper would absorb vibration as no other material could. Alternatively, instant and moderately durable buildings could be made, to be helicoptered into disaster areas, or the bodywork of lightweight electric cars for cities (papier mâché was used for the nose cones of fighter planes during the last war), and so on.

With the clever new machines that we have taught to do our daily work for us in a matter of seconds, dealing with the resulting increase in leisure time is proving an embarrassing problem. Papier mâché is one craft we can take up and one which may find itself precisely in step with the times again. It is tempting to write a long list of its virtues; enough to say that it is wonderfully good-natured stuff, due for a renaissance.

Setting up a work area

The minimum you need is really no more than a quiet corner of your own somewhere near a window, with a table, a chair and a light placed on either side of you, shielded in such a way that at no time do you glimpse a naked bulb. A wooden box about 60 cm (2 ft) square enables you to vary the height of the model and work from more than one viewpoint.

Perfect for modelling heads on, is a piece of dowel rod or broom handle about 1 m (3 ft) long. Resting on the ground and gripped between your knees, it revolves easily and leaves both hands free to work.

Work near a window but not facing it, and only paint with colour by daylight, when this is possible. Models painted by electric light can look disappointingly washed out in daylight and those painted by fluorescent light can look horribly crude and overblown next morning.

Keep the working surface clean; rummaging for small tools hidden under the paper spoils the concentration. A large cardboard box beside you encourages you to throw paper away the moment it is finished with.

A small layout pad is the best palette; simply tear off the leaves as they get used up.

If your scissors or knives are blunt then treat yourself to some new ones. If they are not razor sharp they are likely to cause a lot of damage to the model.

You also need a bucket of water and an old towel to rinse your hands in frequently: fingers get sticky and uncomfortable and then, just as you get a piece of paper modelled perfectly in place, you could find that it has preferred to stay stuck to your finger.

Whether you work alone or with other people around is up to you, of course. Sometimes people can say just the right thing at the right time, giving us a whole new surge of interest when we had had just about enough; but whatever they say can be useful, even when it's obvious that they are missing the point.

Stop to clean and clear everything on the table occasionally – if you don't, a moment may come when you feel that everything is slipping out of control.

A note before starting

You may feel quite secure in the knowledge that you're *not* going to start, thank you very much, having just flicked through the book and seen page after page of instructions. If you have enough application to make a Christmas cake or take a carburettor to pieces then you can take a model through its various stages to a successful completion.

I will tell you why I say this.

Working with papier mâché this way uses two memories – that of sight and that of touch. We all know what things 'look' like and 'feel' like because we notice things and handle things all day long. Since childhood we have been building up this stockpile of impressions of how skin and hair, leather, stone, fabric and china, etc, look and feel. Modelling like this triggers off these two memories, and I notice that what happens is that most people, time and time again, surprise themselves at the skill that they can bring to bear on the making of their model. It is these two memories coming into play. Hitherto, since we hadn't had a great deal of need for them, we were largely unconscious that they were there at all.

I am not saying that this work is easy but I *am* saying that you have a lot more going for you than you think and you won't know this until you start.

Modelling for children

Children take to this type of modelling with paper like professionals. You might think that they had done it all their lives. Adults tend to be more tentative, using the papier mâché at first as though it were clay, but children bash straight in, quite fearless. They appreciate the speed at which the whole thing works, the range of effects that they can get; if well organized, they will start a model in the morning and take it home finished at teatime. It *does* need organizing, because they tend to get excited and race ahead. A good introduction is to get them to start by making finger or glove puppets, such as clowns, witches and wizards, frogs, old ladies and gentlemen, kings and queens, very fat men, goats, octopuses, soldiers, cooks, birds, crocodiles, devils.

Buy some plastic hair curlers from Woolworths or your local general store. These come in three sizes and the two smaller sizes fit children's fingers: being aertex, they simply couldn't be more perfectly designed, allowing the puppet to dry from the inside.

A wooden block about 7·5 cm by 10 cm by 5 cm (3 in by 4 in by 2 in) should be available for each child, with a wooden peg (or large nail, made thicker by binding some rag around it) protruding about 5 cm (2 in) above the block set near one end to act as a prop. If you are not able to provide these modelling aids, the neck of a small beer or medicine bottle is almost as good. Slip the hair curler over one end of this and pad it with a little scrap of paper to stop it wobbling about. Tissue paper and Polycell should be prepared and ready (shown on page 39). Children should be shown how to make the tissue paper into wads (page 42). When they have made a few wads and got the hang of it, making them neither too dry nor too wet and soggy, they then can start building up a ball on the hair curler. The first few wads are put on and then, to stop these dropping straight off again, make some small lengths of doubled tissue pieces about 6 cm ($2\frac{1}{2}$ in) long and crisscross them over the wads like pieces of elastoplast. Continue adding these wads and securing them when necessary.

Children should start modelling the puppet's nose quite early on so they know the front of the head from the back; encourage them not to make the back of the head too flat. The nose should be good and firm, as should be the whole head. (See section on Heads, page 73.)

Get them to stop at a certain point and clean up, continuing more slowly and carefully as they model up the features. Ears can be pieces of tissue trebled and squashed flat, shaped by folding, and 'elastoplasted' into place. They do tend to drop off.

When complete, dry the heads over with a very hot current of air until the surface tissue is brittle.

They may want to add more detail, or if not they can paint them with emulsion using it as a 'filler' rather than as a paint.

A good two hours' drying is needed now until the head is firm and too hard for accidental damage. The children either should go out to play or, if keen to go on, make the hands, if it is a glove puppet, by cutting a hair curler into three parts and using two pieces to model the hands over

(illustrated alongside). There are also hats to prepare, plus hair, glasses (see page 77), walking sticks, and other accessories.

As large as possible a range of 'hair' should be available – coarse string, wool, wood shavings, wire wool, felt, rag, raffia, fur, straw, anything. Polystyrene is useful to have about, as is self-hardening modelling clay. Also cork, sand, dried peas (for warts). The simplest glove for the puppet could be made from a handkerchief with holes cut at the right places for the head and hands, with lace and jewellery, etc, stuck on as appropriate.

Some finger puppets are very effective in a play if the operator wears a neutral-coloured glove and if the head, with little or no neck, is just stuck on the end of a finger.

A play might arise quite naturally out of the varied characters and animals created, and that might be more enterprising than making puppets for an existing play.

Once children can see the number of things that can be made, they will usually provide their own ideas after that; although only one or two may ever go on to develop this papier mâché work, it will always remain a useful item in their repertoire of 'how to make things'.

A small group of six-year-olds from the Rudolph Steiner School, Edinburgh. New to this type of modelling they managed to get the heads modelled in two hours. After the models were dried and emulsioned overnight the children painted and finished them off in two hours the following afternoon. Children should have a wide variety of things to choose from for making clothes, hair and accessories. They work at such an enthusiastic speed that they can get frustrated if they cannot carry out their ideas instantly

Glove puppet

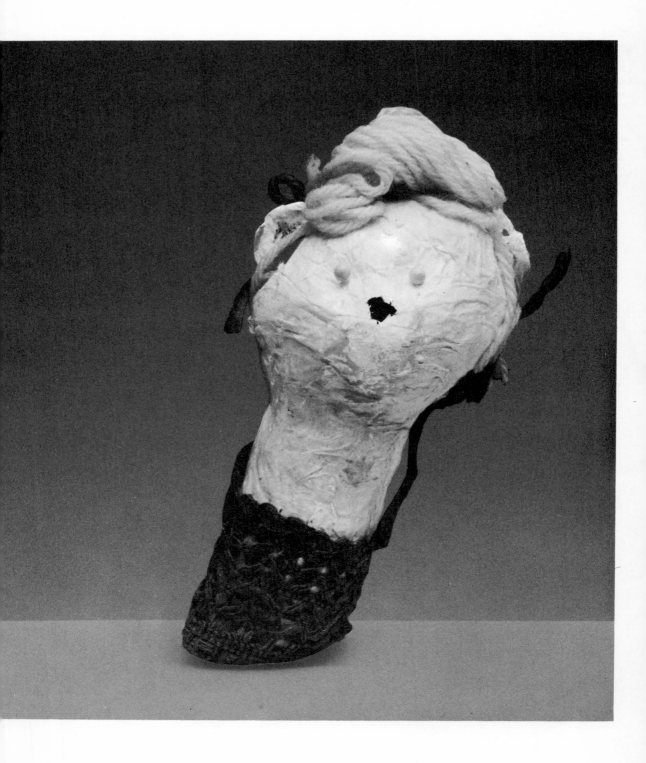

32

The duet: piano made from polystyrene, curved slightly to give a false perspective; ornamentation is plaster-soaked bandage, dried peas and a christmas card

33

Master and mistress: two eighteenth-century figures.
Most of the references for this modelled scene come from Hogarth's
Marriage à la Mode. Note that paintings and drawings from the
period tend to make more authoritative sources of reference than later
reconstructions. As he is depicting his own period the artist puts in
observations that a later artist, thinking them odd and unnecessary,
might edit out.

The figures and their settings were made up as follows:
Fireplace: polystyrene, drinking straws, dried peas and modelling clay
Drapes: good quality linen, stiff enough for the folds not to collapse
when wet with paste, in this case a policeman's shirt was used
Frame: thin cord and very thin strips of bandage soaked in plaster of
Paris

Master: wig – strands of floor mop; scarf – tissue paper; coat and shoes – thick brown paper; stockings and waistcoat – typing paper
Mistress: hair – copper strands of fuse wire; dress – tissue paper

35

Carpet: velvet daubed with emulsion
Grate (detail): card, matchsticks,
modelling clay and real coal (one of
the few things that looks as real in
miniature as normal size)
Dogs: modelling clay

Mantelpiece (detail): books from
card and tissue paper; Staffordshire
dog from modelling clay, varnished

Making a model

From the start we need a clear idea of the model we want. Usually better ideas occur to us as we work and we can alter the model as we go along.

Start with a figure plus some small related objects:

an old lady, blown along by a terrific wind
a clown balancing crockery on a pole
a fat gentleman sitting on a shooting stick
a witch cooking something horrible in a pot
a chef carrying an enormous wedding cake (about to trip over a sleeping cat)
a Scotsman playing bagpipes
a lady wearing a huge flowered hat and lacy summer dress
a model of yourself, wearing the clothes you have on at the moment

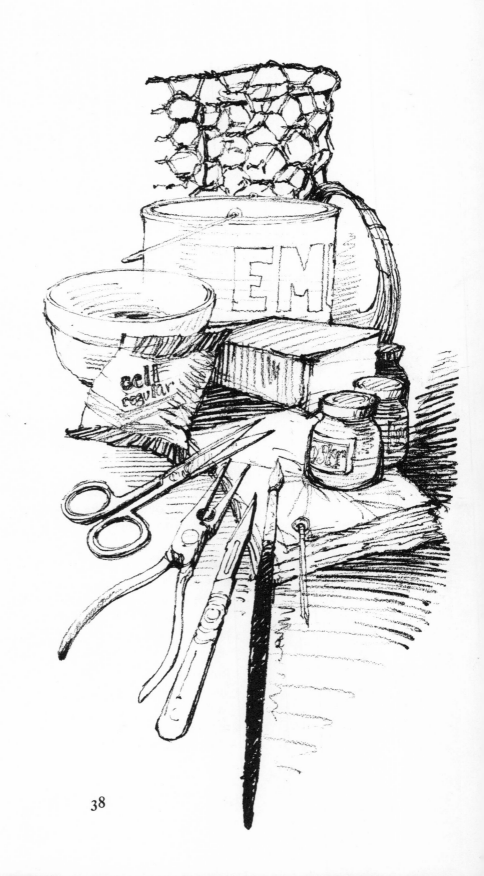

38

Tools and materials

Most of these may be in the house already:

small packet of Polycell wallpaper paste
pudding bowl or plastic dish
block of wood about 10 cm by 15 cm by 5 cm (4 in by
    6 in by 2 in)
one large nail, hammer, a metre (3 ft) of thin wire, a pair
    of electrician's pliers and a pair of sharp scissors
three packets of white tissue paper and six sheets of
    typing paper
a little plasticine or self-hardening modelling material
some small-gauge chicken wire, about twice the size of
    this book
a small paint brush, five pots of poster paint (basic
    colours), some white emulsion and a small tin of
    varnish
a small table vice is useful, but not essential
a scalpel is invaluable

Directions

Sprinkle half the Polycell into 0.25 litres (half a pint) of
water in the bowl. Stir. Five minutes later stir again. Leave
for at least twenty minutes.

Meanwhile, bang the nail firmly into the block of wood,
just off-centre. This will be one leg of the model and may
need to go in at a slight angle according to the model's pose.

*Hammer in the nail at a slight angle,
but not so deep that it cannot be
prised out later*

Armature

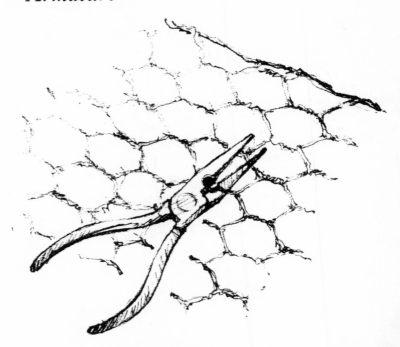

Cut the wire where it is doubled

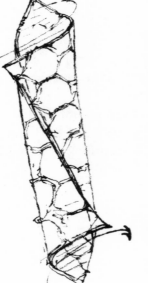

Cut the chicken wire, roll it into a tube. By bending and squeezing with the pliers form the head and body and one leg. Protect your hands if you need to.

Bind the leg to the nail by wrapping it round and round the nail, not allowing the ankle to become too thick.

Cut 23 cm (9 in) of thin wire and secure it to the shoulders, having two lengths extended as arms. Add a length to the hip for the second leg.

It does not matter how rough it looks as long as it is fairly firm and has the shape of the figure.

Spend some time now, twisting and bending this armature into a good, exaggerated and characteristic pose.

Note: if I say that the armature is not too important there will be some raised eyebrows. Obviously, nobody can work with an armature so ill-made that it flops over or falls to bits but, when the armature is covered in papier mâché and dried, it has no further function than to secure the arms to the body and the body to the stand – the dried papier

mâché will be stronger than the armature anyway. Also, one of the advantages of this method is that we can alter, at any time, the position of our figure. He can stand up or sit down, bend over, raise one arm or another until we find a really telling posture. Too solid an armature may inhibit this plasticity, and, lastly, armatures are not very interesting, so why waste time on them?

Making the armature was one of the worst jobs, as sore fingers will testify, but now it is finished. Tear the tissue paper into 10 cm by 5 cm (4 in by 2 in) pieces and stack it into a pile next to the paste, which by now is like jelly. Lightly scoop a little paste on the tips of three fingers of your writing hand and pick up the top tissue.

Fold it and screw it, using both hands, into a fairly tight ball or pad and press firmly on to the chest of the model. The idea is that we want the tissue paper pasted only in patches. As we fold and screw the paper it picks up paste from the fingers in some places but not in others: too much paste and the tissue paper becomes sodden and slimy; too little and the screwed ball begins to spring open again.

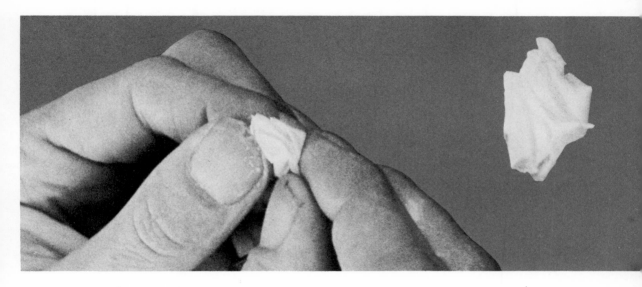

This process of making the tips of the fingers sticky and folding and screwing the paper into an untidy ball or pad is the basic motion of preparing tissue paper to build up the model. We build and add and smooth off, working round the figure, building up the shape. If the model feels too wet, add pieces of drier tissue. If too dry, pieces will fall off. Secure these by putting glued strips over them, like strips of elastoplast.

Take longer pieces of tissue and wind them bandage-fashion around the arms and legs, letting the paper take up glue from the fingers in the same way. Keep the model's wrists and ankles thin. The hands are made separately. Do not put too much definition in the head for the moment. Just indicate the eye sockets, nose and chin.

The model has probably reached a point where it needs to dry now. Put it on the plate rack of a gas stove over a gas flame that is not fierce, but not too gentle either; being very wet it won't catch on fire. A blow heater is also good. The model dries best in a current of hot air. Radiators are too slow except for overnight drying. The inside of the model takes some days to dry, so be content if after half an hour over the gas the surface of the model is dry and hard enough to continue working on.

Hands

While the figure dries, make its hands. Take ten pieces of tissue 1.5 cm by 2.5 cm (3 in by 1 in). Fold as in the diagram with your fingers only lightly pasted. Of the ten fingers made, choose the two thickest for thumbs, and place four fingers each next to the thumbs. Use your own hand as a guide to which finger is longer than another. Take care not to make two left or two right hands.

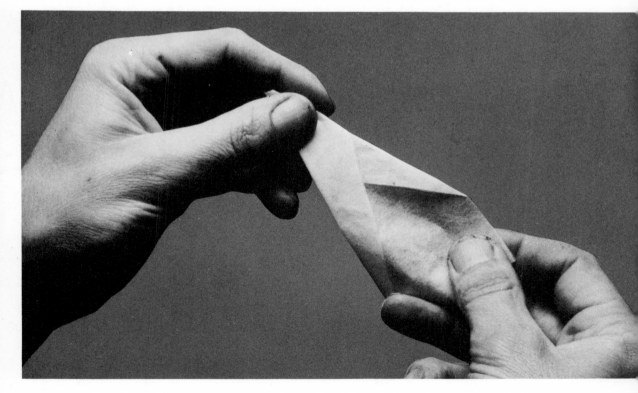

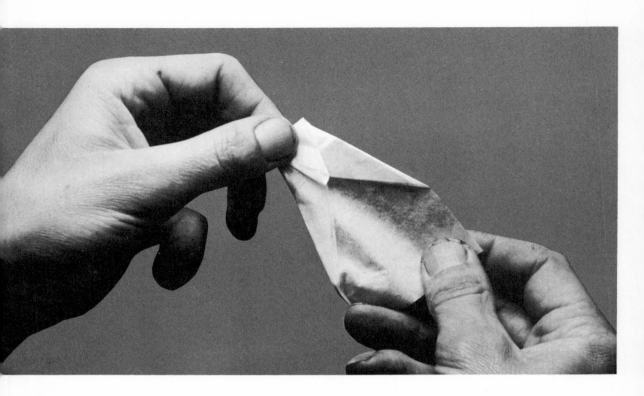

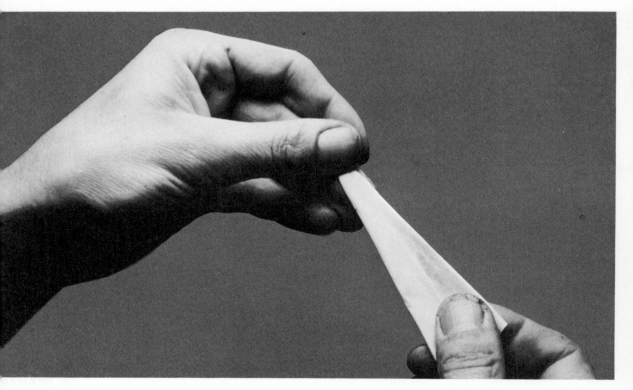

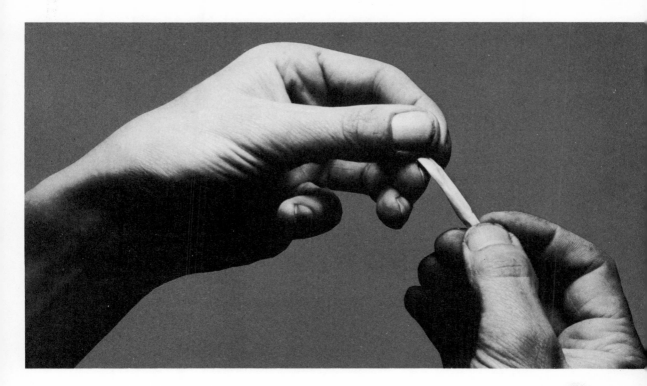

Take these five fingers in your hand and wrap sticky tissue around the base of the knuckles and between the thumb. Don't attempt to shape the fingers too much now or they may begin to come apart. Hang over the gas to dry. Let the two hands become semi-dry before shaping. If the hand is too bulky when clenched, snip off the tops of the fingers or cut one finger out entirely. Bind the hands to the model's wrist with more sticky tissue. They may look rather large. If so, it is all to the good. Slightly oversized hands often suit a model.

If these hands still look wrong, just leave them. You can work on them later.

Model the front and back of the head at the same time.

Use the tissue in the same way as before but now in much smaller pieces. A nail file or small knife is useful for pressing and smoothing surfaces. Eyes set well back in their sockets are shadowed and more alive.

47

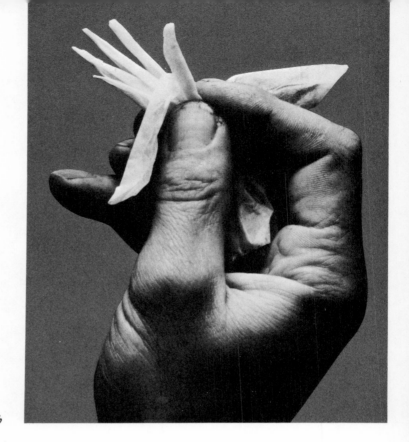

Securing the thumb

Hand ready for drying

The chapter on Heads, page 73, may be of some help.

We should now have the head modelled, hands in position and feet shaped.

Dry for an hour.

When dry the model has probably become wrinkled and stained. In fact it looks so incredibly dreary and disappointing that you may feel like strangling it. Do, and at the same time remind it that if it wasn't for you it would still be just a few old bits of waste paper lying about; they soon toe the line after that, you'll find. You are about halfway to finishing, and if the first half wasn't much fun, the second more than makes up for it.

Next you become a tailor and need a sharp pair of scissors and some typing or exercise-book paper. Good-quality writing paper may be too stiff. Dress the model in the same order as that which it would have used if it had dressed itself that morning.

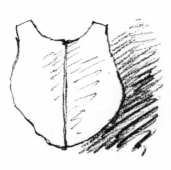

Shirt front

Cut out the shirt front from typing paper with a crease down the centre (it looks like a waiter's dickie), and paste it firmly on to the model's breast.

Collar and cuffs

Take the neck measurement with a piece of cotton. Cut out the collar shape. Smear the inside with paste. Fold. Smear the neck of the model and press the collar into place. Put on the cuffs in the same way.

Trousers

Cut out each leg, paste it and crease. Paste the leg and press on the trouser so that the crease comes to the front and untidy joins go to the back. Move trousers about as little as possible once they are on. Keep any folds that look natural, smooth out any that don't. Cut out a new pair of trousers if the first pair need too much adjusting and have lost their crispness.

Waistcoat

Cut out the shape. Paste inside the waistcoat and the model's chest and press in place. Pull the waistcoat taut across the tummy if the model is fat.

Jacket

Work on the sleeves first; they go almost over the cuffs at one end and are moulded to the shoulders at the other. If the arm is very bent, straighten it, add the sleeve and gently

50

bend it back. If it is very close to the body, wait until the rest of the jacket is on before bending back into position.

Stick two pieces of typing paper together by brushing them evenly and lightly with the paste and press the two sticky sides together, squeezing out any air bubbles.

You need to cut three separate pieces for the jacket. The complete back and the left and right front. Leave out the collar and lapels for the moment and mark out the three separate pieces for the jacket. Cut them out with *sharp* scissors.

Score a line alongside, and very close to, all the outside edges with a ballpoint pen. This indentation in the soft paper will suggest a seam and although it seems a lot of extra bother for a very small result, it does take away the utility look of the clothes, playing its part later in the exquisiteness of the finished model.

Smear the body of the model and the insides of the jacket panels with a little of the paste and place all three lightly in position. Press them firmly only when you are satisfied that they all hang correctly. Blend the three pieces into one complete jacket by smoothing over the joins.

Take a moment or two to slightly curl some of the jacket's edges in such a way as to give them a 'well-worn' look. With this small consideration we add another dimension to the model – time.

Paste small pieces of typing paper over any nasty gaps. Allow the bottom of the jacket to hang away from the body and flap outwards or backwards as a real one would if a person were in motion.

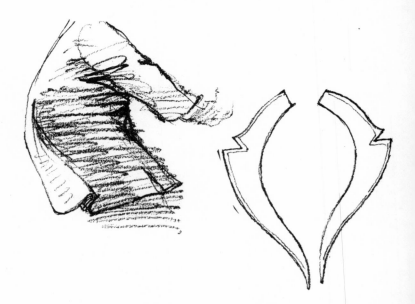

Dry for a quarter of an hour if the pieces look insecure.

Add the collar and lapels in two pieces, as shown, plus pocket flaps, ties, handkerchiefs, etc.

Hats

By now, you are better able to judge what paper to use. Very thin card would work for a top hat or a wide hat brim. Build the hat up on the head, adding hair afterwards.

Cloaks and skirts

These are made up in sections. It helps to push thin pieces of wood or wire into the model to support the cloak or skirt as it dries. It is worth taking trouble to get the feeling of movement, particularly with the old lady in the wind. (Has she a tight hold on her hat? Are we treated to a glimpse of petticoat?)

Pre-shaped and pre-folded pieces of doubled typing paper pressed on to the pasted model. Temporary pieces of wire or wood will hold them in position while they dry, when they can then support their own weight

To suggest heavy folds that reach the ground (such as period dresses or heavy curtains) take the pre-shaped piece of paper and, just before pressing it into place on the model, sharply tap it once on the table whilst holding it upright, and so force in creases at its base

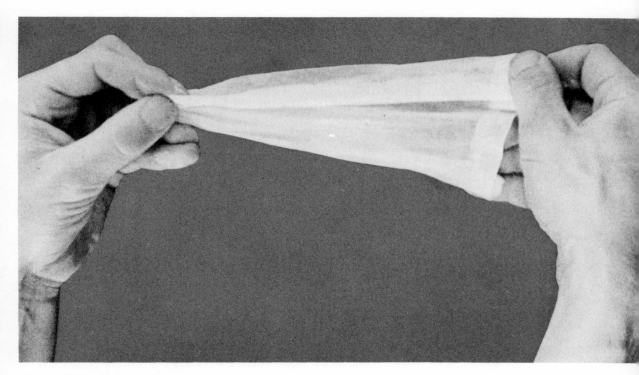

Shaping folds of a dress prior to pressing it on to the model

Props

Self-hardening modelling material is perfect for small extras like the chef's cake, the cat, crockery, etc. Plasticine is all right but needs gluing into position with Evo–Stik or Copydex.

Odd effects

Use a paper doily smeared with paste for a summer dress or parasol. Dried and split peas, rice and lentils glued on make a good texture. Tiny electrical components always seem to come in useful, as do seeds and burrs, pieces of broken fountain pen and odd bits of jewellery. Woolworths nearly always seem to have just what you need; you are going to paint the model with white emulsion, it will be impossible to tell from what these various items were originally made.

The model should be dried again now, in a warm air current overnight.

Clean away any sticky bits of tissue paper from the table and floor, or they will dry like rock.

Painting

With a soft No 6 or No 8 brush, preferably an inexpensive ox-hair one, paint the model with white emulsion. You are not really *just* painting, you are using the emulsion, which is quite thick, to fill up gaps, to smooth off surfaces that have wrinkled in the drying, and to blend one piece of the model to another. In some places the wrinkles may have been lucky accidents, for instance around the eyes or mouth, so give them just one thin coat. The jacket or dress usually needs several coats before a clean smooth surface begins to appear. It is unwise to paint the face too heavily, as the detail gets drowned. Hands usually need plenty of filling. When dry, after an hour or so over the gas, the model really looks fresh and 'together'. In fact you are definitely beginning to feel much better about the whole thing.

With fine sandpaper gently smooth off places like the nose, forehead and cheeks.

Throughout history, hardly anybody has painted on top of sculpture successfully. After we have painted ours we will probably see why. The difficulty comes if you consider the 'colouring' separately from the 'modelling'. They have to work together, with the modelling going so far and the colour taking over from there. Unless you are sensitive to this you'll just get 'painted sculpture' or, even worse, painting working *against* the sculpture and so giving a contradictory effect. Painting, in this case, is largely tinting and suggesting, especially in the face.

56

(To put it bluntly, it is the difference between the make-up of a beautiful and natural woman and that of a blousey old stripper.)

Start with the face. Add poster or water colour to white emulsion to get a light, warm, creamy ochre, the colour of a very light-brown chicken egg, and paint all the exposed skin areas, including the hands. Leave to dry. Meanwhile mix up plenty of colour for the jacket, trousers, dress, etc, and paint them from all angles. Paint the back of the model as thoroughly as the front. If the face is now dry, mix a delicate watery pink and lay the model on its back while you paint on this tint. As one wash dries add more to the nose, cheeks and ears. If your wash is too pink your model will have apoplexy. A good pink is obtained with crimson and yellow cooled down with the tiniest touch of green. Painting the face has to be done as delicately as possible. Don't forget the hands.

It is rare that anyone can paint something perfectly the first time, particularly large areas like coats and dresses. So, if you are not happy, mix up more colour and paint on top. (If you let tiny specks of the original colour show through, it tends to make the second colour less flat, more alive, and the contrast is too minute to be noticeable.)

A can of gold spray is very helpful. You can mask off the face and hands with tissue paper, and spray the dress gold, painting a pattern on top when dry, or give the finished painted model a very, very light spray, masking off unsuitable areas. If painting black, add crimson – it makes the black richer. Use paint thickly as this helps to get clean edges where one colour comes up against another. Painting hair is usually done best with several washes of similar colour. With a fine brush add details like eyebrows, moustaches, patterns on ties and dresses, buttons, etc.

Finally – if you have some varnish (picture varnish is best) put a dab on the nose and cheeks if it suits them to be shiny and varnish boots and shoes, or buttons and belts, or hair, but don't thoughtlessly varnish the *whole* model or most of its delicacy will disappear and it will simply look wooden.

I hope that you feel like adding a lot of extras. It is this detail that delights people who see it later, as they feel that they have discovered it for themselves. Everything we add tells more and more about the figure; he has odd socks on, for example, or pens and pencils, or a pipe in his top pocket, a handkerchief half in and half out of his pocket, or his tie is slack.

Clean off the base and sandpaper it. Varnish or paint flat black. If it is too scruffy, cut a new base and drill in a nail-size hole. Half fill the hole with glue. Carefully prise the nail and model from its old stand and drop it into the new hole. Position and support the model whilst the glue dries.

If the model was a success there is a section on page 97 which deals with making a stand and a glass case to protect it from its worst enemy, dust.

1 *Wire armature with the desk cut from featherlite board (available from some good art suppliers, used mainly for architectural models). Note that some of the surfaces are slightly curved to soften and integrate the desk with the model*

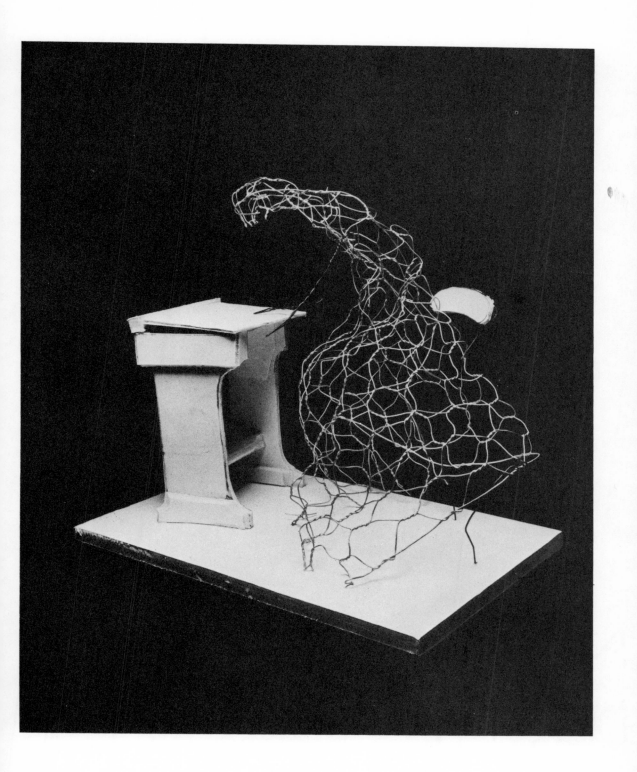

2   *Dress made of typing paper.*
Paper doilies were used to give some
texture to the desk and then heavily
coated in emulsion. Cat made of
modelling clay

3   *The dress was given three or four*
coats of emulsion to give it the feel of
heavy, good-quality material, the
final coat being a faded-pink colour.
The hair is of strands of double tissue
wound round the end of a fine paint
brush and pulled out slightly like a
spring. The desk is tinted with
watered-down coloured inks and the
finished model spattered with gold
spray (this spattering effect is
achieved by barely depressing the little
plastic spray unit on top of the can so
that it works inefficiently. Practise
first)

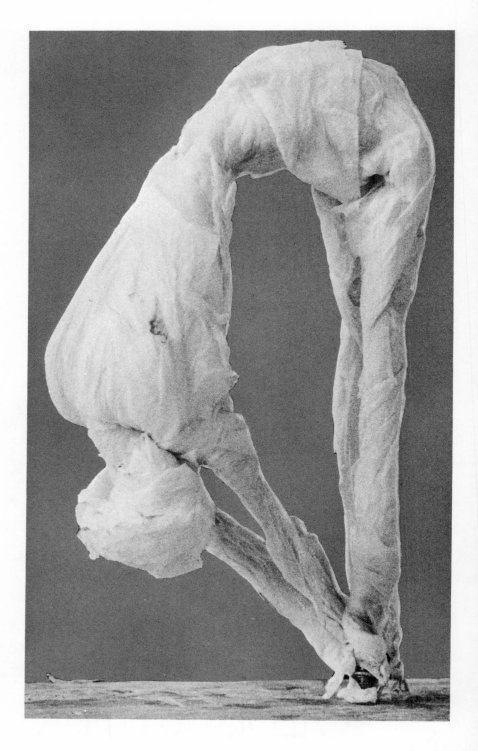

Figure at a stage where it can be tempting to give up. Usually drying it thoroughly is the answer

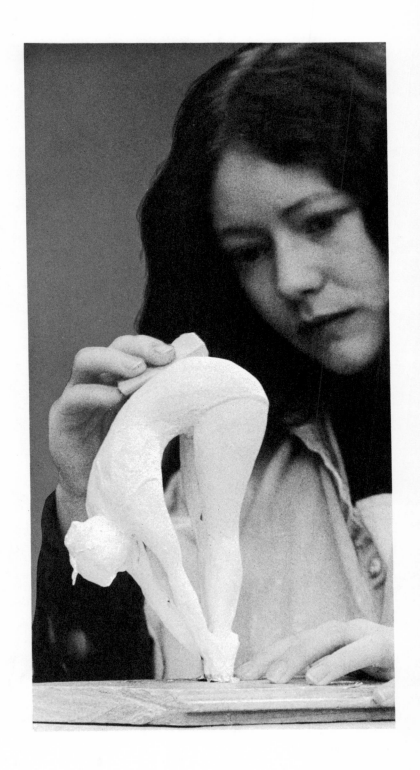

Dress from typing and tissue paper

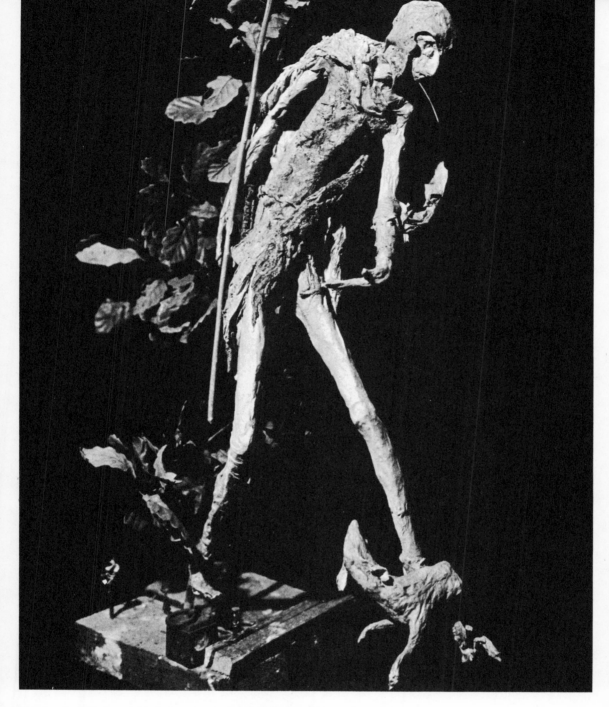

Nun on horseback, made of tissue and typing paper

Soldier kicking dog. Finished model painted with ferrous oxide and left outside to rust. Background made of real beech leaves

*Ballet figure. Legs and face sanded
down with fine sandpaper, painted
with emulsion, and sanded again*

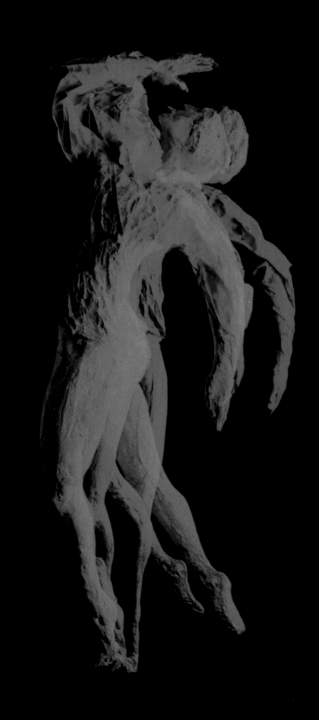

70

Beau: with a knitting needle stick

Lord Longford dripping with slime (model first appeared in the Sunday Telegraph Magazine)

Idi Amin (model first appeared in the Sunday Telegraph Magazine)

*Victorian hamster: modelled in tissue
paper with clothes of typing paper*

*Life-size Jersey cow: chicken wire on
a wooden frame; skin – brown paper
and a velveteen tablecloth; eyes –
rubber ball cut in two halves*

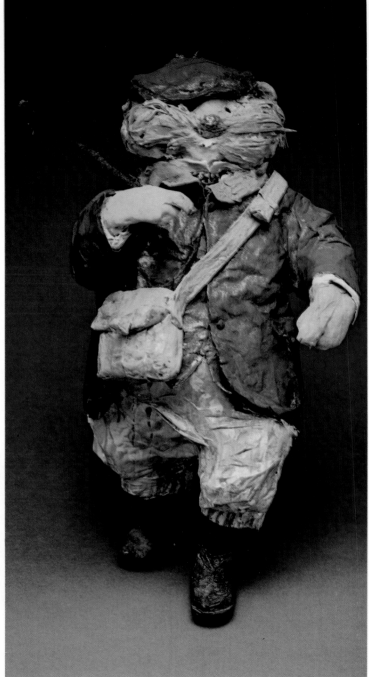

Modelling heads

Shape the chicken wire as shown alongside – leaving a small piece of wire extended to take the nose.

Start with a hard triangular wad of sticky tissue paper for the nose and make this the right size and shape now, if possible, so that it doesn't have to be altered later. This gives you something to 'key' the face on to and helps you begin visualizing the face in your mind's eye.

Model the face along the lines illustrated here – which roughly follow the muscles of the face.

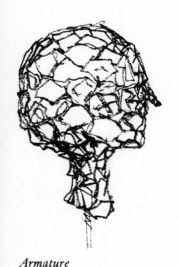

Armature

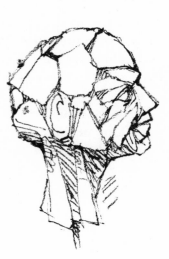

A rough guide to follow in building up the face muscles

Set the eye sockets well back in the head and try and get the 'feel' of the face you are modelling, that is, whether it is fine and pointed or bland or heavy, etc.

For bony areas such as the forehead, cheekbone and jaw, pack the tissue paper in hard tight wads. Make slightly softer lengths for muscles and finish off with very small pieces of tissue paper laid on as skin.

Be careful not to cover the whole face with this skin and so risk losing some of the modelling which may be just right as it is.

Usually the head is completed in three stages. The first stage is roughing in the whole head, including the back (don't make this too flat, by the way).

Dry the surface very quickly over a fierce flame.

The second stage is altering and adding to the head until it is close to being finished. It is then given a chance to dry over a current of hot air until there is no longer any danger of pieces dropping off. This gives you a chance to clear up and get ready for stage three which is adding detail, painting with thick emulsion where you need smoothness and with watered-down emulsion where you would like to keep the wrinkles; also, cutting and trimming with a scalpel knife.

When the emulsion is bone dry, fine down with sand-paper areas where a silky smoothness is essential. It is possible to get a finish like porcelain if you are painstaking enough.

Suggestions for tinting and colouring the head are given on page 56.

Take the advantage of the facility that this kind of modelling gives you to squeeze, elongate or flatten the head, even when it is quite near to being finished; don't be frightened of pulling the head to pieces and re-modelling if you are quite sure it hasn't developed in a way that you are happy with.

Use the emulsion as a filler to get rid of deep gaps that shouldn't be there, and even add a little Polyfilla to thicken the emulsion if necessary.

An exercise in discipline is to make yourself model the

back of the head as thoroughly as the face, so turn the model around often as you work or it will only look right from the front.

When you achieve a piece of modelling that you are particularly pleased with, don't fiddle with it, *leave it alone!*

Eyes

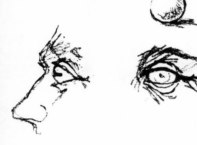

Eyeball and eyelid

Roll out two small balls of plasticine or modelling clay and push them gently, well into the eye sockets. Two eyelid-shaped pieces above and below secure them in place. Push in two deep holes with a matchstick to make pupils and manœuvre the eyeballs so that the two eyes work together and have the right expression.

The upper eyelid should protrude well over the eyeball, throwing a shadow over the eye. Eyes can look a bit 'starey' without this.

In a smaller head it is a good idea to leave out the eyeballs altogether, leaving a deep cavity behind the eyelids; this results in the eyes being more suggestive and alive.

The corner of a piece of tissue paper pushed into the outer corner of the eye and pressed gently to the side of the head suggests beautifully the wrinkles that collect in the corner of the eye.

Two small marbles might work well for eyeballs, or pinheads pushed into the pupil, so that occasionally they just catch the light.

Mouth

As you look in the mirror you will see how your own mouth is formed and you should model a simplified version of the muscles that make it up.

Put on the teeth before making the mouth, if they are

75

to show. After modelling the mouth (illustrated alongside) put in the sheaves of muscles that lead from the outer nostril and swing out around the corner of the mouth.

If you have to alter the mouth when it has dried a little, pulling the corners up and out to make it smile or laugh, these muscles round the mouth will also stretch, and the whole area around the mouth will take up the 'laugh'.

The thing that can make models look slightly horrific is if the mouth is laughing but nothing else in the face is (like a bank manager's smile).

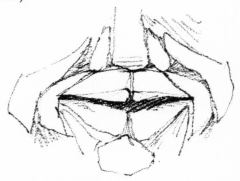

Two pieces of tissue pushed flat into the mouth and pressed against the upper and lower lip sometimes form small creases on the lips that are uncannily lifelike. Give a very sharp, clear definition to the upper lip if it is suitable for the type of face you are creating.

Hair

Whatever you make the hair from, it is best put on starting from the lower back to the front of the head, the same way tiles are put on a roof.

Tissue paper can be spun into fine hair but it can get tiresome putting it on one hair at a time. It is quicker to model with large wads of tissue and only put the fine hair where it is most telling.

Cover the head well in Polycell and press the hair into it. Trim with scissors when dry.

Putting on hair

76

Glasses

Pull out some strands of copper or silver wire from a piece of electric flex. Make a generous guess as to the length of wire needed and twist as many strands together as will make them up to the thickness needed for the frames. Take two of these lengths and twist them together in the centre, twist them around the handle of a paint brush or anything of the right circumference (as in the diagram); twist them together again, and bend the wire with a pair of small pliers. Insert the ends into a small hole at the ear and glue them into position. By using fine wire you get a suggestion of spectacles which is just as effective, if not more so, than modelling them in detail.

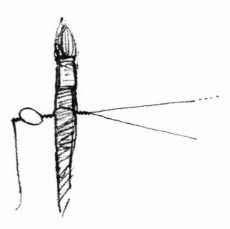

Caricature

From your experience with your first model it will be easy to appreciate how well this method of papier mâché lends itself to caricature; caricature is its nature.

Our job, then, is to try to understand a little more clearly the essence of caricature and not to get carried away by the sheer fun of exaggeration. When sitting in trains or round a table, look at a face and try to visualize it 'growing'. That is, developing forwards and backwards along the lines that the different features are already tending to go, expanding or contracting one feature at a time.

Small eyes retract to pinpricks, a domed forehead swells to a balloon. A thin small mouth becomes a hair-crack. Pink ears become fluorescent. If you can do this, even a little, it helps to break up your usual 'fixed' picture of a face into something more mobile and plastic. Then select from the four or five possibilities perhaps two around which to centre the caricature. If you try to exaggerate them all, they will tend to cancel each other out. Some features remain neutral, just playing their part in aiding the 'likeness'.

The most important overall quality that you must be aware of is the 'texture' of the person. Are they smooth, monochromed like metal, or rough and dry-textured like a cottage wall? Oily or flaky? Taut or relaxed? Neat, alert and birdlike, or an easy-going shambles? Noisy or peaceful; outward going or inward looking? This quality is likely to be echoed in line, shape, texture and colour throughout the body, from the hair to the choice of clothes, and also externally from type of furnishings right through to make of car and breed of dog.

Lastly, it would be useful to know a little about how and where the various characteristics that we know of the person display themselves. From my own observations, discrimination in a face is located at the eyebrow and the muscles that operate it. Intelligence and humour (closely related) are in the outer corner of the eye, coupled with the shadow from the eyelid. It is a pity to miss this.

The nose indicates the kind of interest a person takes in the world around him; the muscles that lead to the base of the nostrils show quite clearly a person's attitude to himself, particularly marked in self-satisfied, vain or fastidious people. Lips show how much and under what conditions a person behaves generously. Sexuality displays itself in the cheekbone and outer muscles of the neck; the chin might indicate tenacity. Seediness gives itself away at the hair behind the ear and disappointment, at the jowls. The back of the neck seems to be a display point for some characteristic that a person is largely unconscious of, possibly connected with inner growth, or lack of of it.

One last word on caricature that is worth remembering: some people find it odious. Perhaps they feel that life is quite bizarre enough already without deliberately 'aggravating' it; they may prefer quietly to overlook a person's idiosyncrasies and contradictions. Happily, many more people enjoy it, seeing their own privately formed observations confirmed.

If the caricature is truthfully, remorselessly but sympathetically done, without vindictiveness, then it embodies a good deal of truth from which everyone can learn, not least the sitter. Features like smugness, pomposity, lewd-ness, cunning, servility, humourlessness, indolence and the like, need to be lampooned and it is interesting that genuine qualities like intelligence, innocence, compassion and courage defy parody: the joke backfires. You could try a caricature model of yourself. That might make quite a vivid introduction.

Methods

Essentially, the same processes are used for the caricature as for the first model. If you choose to do a large head or a miniature body, the placing of the nail has to be well considered beforehand, and be quite secure.

On a miniature body, the size of the hands vary according to their position and importance, but generally speaking they should be miniature if held at the sides, and increase rapidly in size as they come up to the level of the face.

It is best to model the whole figure altogether, although there is a strong temptation to model the head first and attach a body later. When modelling the head, as in straight portraiture, it is important to have a clear feel of the person right from the application of the first piece of papier mâché on to the wire armature.

When the figure is almost completely modelled but still damp, it is then possible to manœuvre the head about radically. The nose can be pulled and extended right out, or the head crushed downward like a toad, or the sides of the head squeezed together. If the head has been well constructed – that is, the muscles modelled on the same principle as actual ones – it is possible for it to survive these distortions (after a bit of patching up) and still be very believable as a head; only now it will be far bolder and more extreme than we could have visualized initially.

There is usually something that will mimic hair perfectly, coarse string combed out, wire wool, wood shavings, etc, which may need a light painting or spraying to blend them with the rest of the model. Use real objects where appropriate; artificial pearls, matchsticks or scalpel blades for teeth, for example, and real false eyelashes. Also, you might consider placing the figure in a historical or mythological setting. It may well 'suit' your subject to be portrayed as an eighteenth-century fop, a Pan, Boudicca, Harlequin, a Victorian explorer, etc. Particularly effective would be to metamorphize the person into a peacock or hawk; a lion, snake or mouse; even a pig!

Finish off by adding pertinent objects such as a piece of furniture, a typewriter, a miniature building, a musical instrument, golf clubs, as a final comment.

Charles de Gaulle, about 30 cm (12 in) high

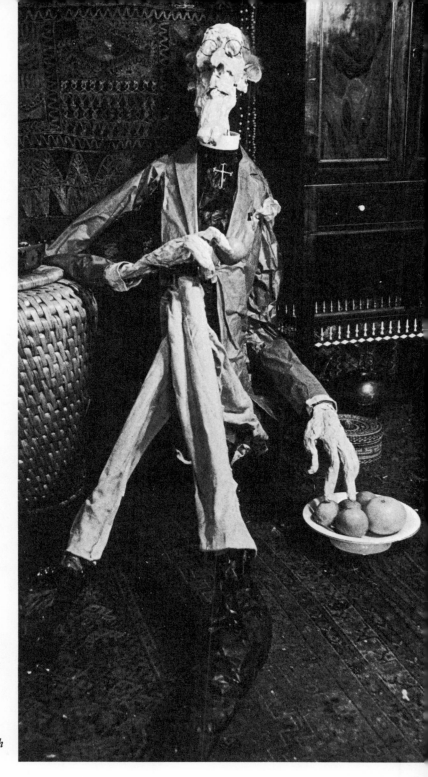

HRH The Prince of Wales (unpainted)

Vicar, 4.25 m (14 ft), modelled in brown paper, trousers of sacking, teeth of yellow soap

Small caricature model of the harpist Graham Bell. The harp is cut out of polystyrene and the base made from a block of wood bound round with string, painted, and spattered with gold spray

Making animals

Armature

The method of making these animals is very similar to making a figure. The armature is best made from small-gauge chicken wire on a piece of plank about 30 cm (12 in) long with a hole drilled in the centre. A length of soft wire to support the chicken wire is fixed firmly in this hole. The wire is only to support the chicken wire and should be as simple as possible, because as you make the model you may have a much better idea for it and want to alter its position, and too well-made an armature might make this difficult. Wire coat hangers are about the right thickness but are too stiff and springy – use them if you cannot find any softer wire; the perfect thing is aluminium armature wire but this is not easy to find, except in some craft shops.

Model the animal as quickly as you can and get it into a good, lively, characteristic posture. You might like to make two animals fighting or playing – a lot more work but well worth it.

Build up the animal using tissue paper for the muscles

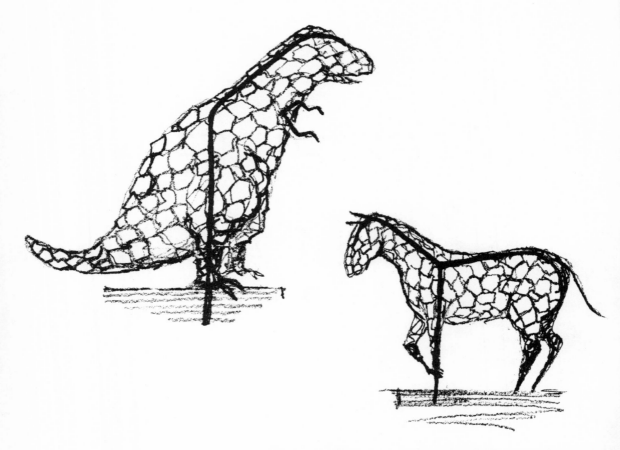

but where you want soft folds of loose skin use paper hand–kerchiefs or kitchen roll. Thin brown paper is very good for tough, wrinkled skin where the skin is flexible.

There are hundreds of things that you can use to make the animal's texture. Scales, for instance, can be made from small, stiff green leaves, from seeds, or cut from card.

A good knobby, warty effect can be got by using rice, lentils or split peas, anything like that. A hunt through the larder should produce just the right thing.

Crocodile skin can be emulated with small rough pieces of bark. These are stuck on the model by coating the animal in thick Polycell, pressing them on and allowing to dry. After they have been painted with thick emulsion it's almost impossible to see what they are so you should feel free to use anything you like, absolutely anything. Eggshells put on and gently crushed make good armoured skin. Fur can be built up with fine pieces of tissues, possibly some soft cloth, imitation-velvet or even real fur. Real fur has to be sprayed gently with spray paint several times first to make it stiff, then it can be painted with emulsion. Snake-skin can be suggested by cutting up a fine-meshed nylon 'onion-bag' and sticking pieces on. Fine sand sprinkled on to the wet glue will also work. When dry, different grasses can be ideal for making crests, plumes or whiskers.

Painting

The notes on painting a model on page 56 apply here too. When painting an animal you can be quite bold in getting the effect that you want; cans of spray paint and small jars of fluorescent poster paint are useful.

A good effect for crocodiles can be caught by polishing the finished model with light-brown boot polish. Matt varnish is another way of finishing it off. Having made your animal, put it in a natural setting such as clumps of dried grass, or a cave with bones scattered on a sandy floor.

Making large animals

This demands much the same approach as smaller animals, but everything will be proportionally larger.

The armature has to be made of light wood and so the finished model should be worked out in some detail before-hand as it will be difficult to alter later on. Larger-gauge chicken wire can be used as small-gauge wire, although better, can work out expensive. Larger wads of tissue paper can be used for the finer modelling, with thin brown paper for making muscles. Strips of newspaper make a good tight skin to build upon when thoroughly dry.

You have to use your imagination as to the variety of

textures and the materials required for them, but poly-styrene is especially useful. You can cut, tear or burn the shapes you need.

Paint the animal thickly with emulsion when dry.

The life-size cow (shown on page 72) was made in this way, using a velveteen tablecloth for skin and some old carrots for udders (which later unfortunately sprouted!).

Large models soon lose their freshness and get to look very dogeared unless protected, so give them four or five coats of varnish – the final coat being matt – particularly if they are to go outside.

Dinosaur, 45 cm (18 in) high. Armoured skin is represented by eggshells gently crushed on to the pasted model

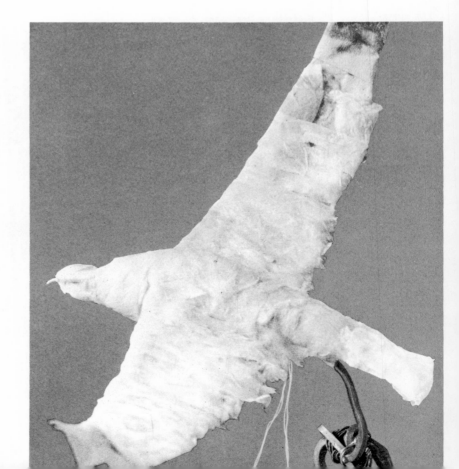

Three stages of a seagull

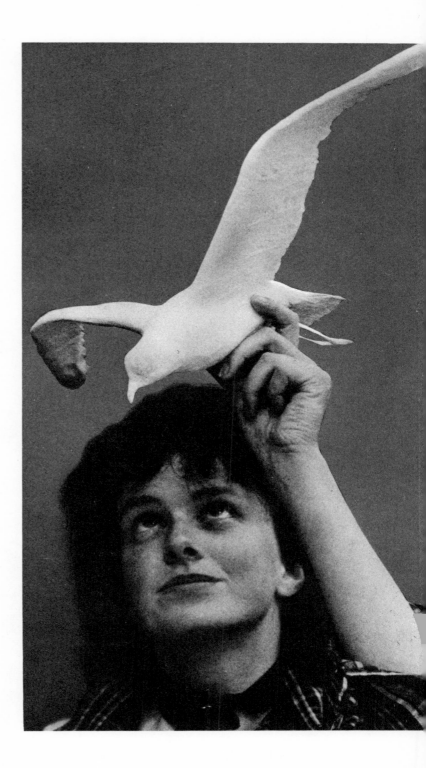

Crocodile, about 60 cm (24 in) long.
The model was thickly smeared with
paste, and encrusted with rough tree
bark, lentils, split peas and rice

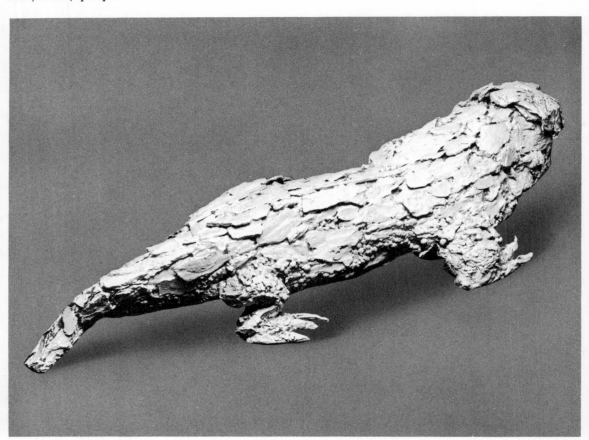

Making a stand

If you want to make a really posh stand for your figure go to a frame-making shop and buy a round, oval or oblong wooden frame: a really well made, good-looking stand is important. It means that you are saying to the world, 'I know it's papier mâché but I think it is a beautiful thing, capable of standing on a shelf alongside carriage clocks and Dresden china. I am proud of it, that is why I have invested money and care on the stand.' Stuck on an old lump of wood, your model will have a 'take it or leave it' sort of appearance.

Place the frame on some stout card and cut out a base. Glue the base card on to the frame with latex paper glue (Copydex). When dry, paint the whole stand inside and out with emulsion, particularly the inside where the card joins the frame.

95

Bend or splay the wire or nail protruding from the model so that the model will rest level with the top of the stand.

Fill in the frame with plaster of Paris – dental plaster from the chemist is best – and secure the model into position whilst it dries. You may prefer to build up the plaster on the stand into rocks or steps, whatever the model suggests. A pleasing effect for the stand is first to paint it a dark rusty red, then spray on gold paint in several even coats, and when quite dry very gently sand it with fine sandpaper, so that the red just begins to show here and there.

To make a simpler stand: keep the block of wood that the model is on already and cover the four outside edges with latex adhesive. When that is semi-dry, wind good-quality string or fine cord round and round the stand with one layer right next to another, starting at the top of the back. Paint it over with emulsion and spray gold. Clean off and polish or varnish the top.

Making a case

This is not so simple, and it is a shame that the very last job should be so difficult. Under glass a model will keep its colour and freshness for years; unprotected it will fade and, worst of all, collect dust. Even with a feather duster dust will stay in the crevices. Your model will go the way of all unprotected papier mâché and become tired-looking, dogeared and tatty – which is what gives papier mâché a bad name. You may be fortunate enough to come across a glass case which is the right size or even a glass dome from a carriage clock. You can buy plastic domes for carriage clocks imported from Switzerland plus a wooden base to fit, if you know a real clock shop, but they do take some hunting down. It is most likely that you will have to make one of your own.

This requires picture glass cut very accurately (people who like the plasticity of papier mâché aren't usually the same people that can cut glass successfully). Work out the happiest size to fit the model. Too large and it looks lost, too small is claustrophobic.

Carefully measure the depth, length and height. Two thicknesses of glass will be added to the width measurement (see the diagram). This shouldn't make much difference unless the placing of the glass case on the stand is crucial.

Add two thicknesses of glass – 6 mm ($\frac{1}{4}$ in) if it is picture glass – to the width measurement of the top and this *is* crucial, as the top pane has to rest on top of the sides. Buy glass-binding epoxy resin. (Ordinary epoxy resin will do if the other isn't available.) Clean the four edges of the glass with methylated spirit and tissue paper. You need a box roughly the same shape but smaller than the case you intend to make and one with edges at exact right angles. This is to hold the glass panes together as you wait for them to dry.

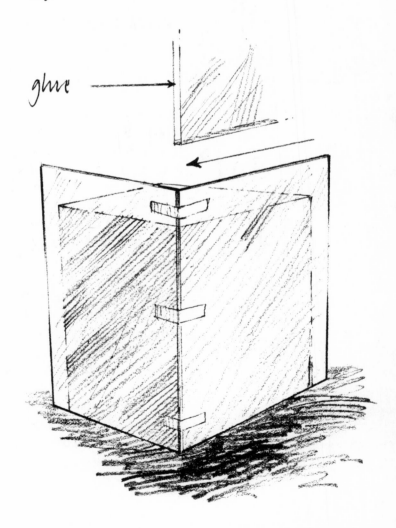

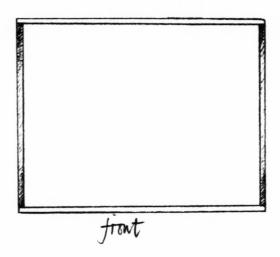

front

Then, with infinite care, glue the edge of one side pane of glass, place the front pane against it (see the diagram) and Sellotape it into position. It is easy to wipe off surplus glue from the outside with warm, soapy water on a soft cloth, but from the inside it is all but impossible, so spread the epoxy very evenly and sparingly. When this is dry according to the makers' instructions, repeat the process with the other side panel. When that is dry, the fourth and last pane is fixed, gluing both edges of the side panes at the same time.

When ready the top is carefully dropped on to the four prepared edges.

There is tremendous satisfaction in doing this carefully and unhurriedly. Go at it impatiently and you will end up furious and distraught, I promise you.

With a fine file, round off the eight sharp corner edges (ie top and sides). A 6 mm ($\frac{1}{4}$ in)-square beading should be glued and pinned around the base of the case, flush to the glass to stop it from slipping about.

Clean inside and out with methylated spirit and tissue (not window polish: the powder will get into gaps in the glue and dry white).

If you have done all that you have quite likely made a family heirloom. Well done, well done indeed.

Glossary

COPYDEX   Light Latex glue often used for gluing fabric.
ELASTOPLAST   Band-Aid.
ELECTRIC FLEX   Electric cord.
EMULSION   Thick, flat, water-based paint.
EVOSTICK   Strong impact-adhesive for household use.
PLASTICINE   Oil-and-clay mix for modelling.
POLYCELL   Cellulose-based wallpaper paste (preferable to flour-based paste, which sticks to the fingers).
POLYFILLA   Cellulose-reinforced plaster used for filling cracks.
SELLOTAPE   Scotch tape.

Index

Papier Mâché

Peter Rush is an illustrator of children's books. Having trained as an artist at St Martin's School of Art in London, he spent three working years in America. Since his return he has become well known through his contributions to the illustrations used on the BBC television programme Jackanory *over the past twelve years. He took to papier mâché originally as a relief from so much drawing, and several of his models have been photographed for the* Sunday Telegraph Magazine. *He now lives in Scotland with his wife and three children.*

Amy Emms' Story of
DURHAM QUILTING

Amy Emms' Story of
DURHAM QUILTING

AMY EMMS MBE

Edited by Pam Dawson

Search Press

First published in Great Britain 1990
Search Press Limited
Wellwood, North Farm Road
Tunbridge Wells, Kent TN2 3DR

First published in paperback 1991

Copyright © Search Press Limited 1990

Designer Julie Wood
Diagrams Marilyn Clarke
Photographs by Search Press Studios on pages 7, 8, 21, 25, 26, 29, 30, 34, 36, 39–41, 44–53, 59, 61, 63, 65, 69, 71, 74, 76–81, 83, 84, 86.

The publishers have endeavoured to obtain, where possible, permission to reproduce the original black-and-white and colour photographs supplied by Amy Emms. The following photographs are reproduced by courtesy of Sunderland and Hartlepool Publishing and Printing Limited, pages 15, 17, 18, 19; Beamish, The North of England Open Air Museum, pages 16, 23; The Tyne and Wear Museums Service, page 27; The Northern Echo, pages 33, 35.

Colour photographs on page 30 by kind permission of Deidre Amsden; on page 85 by kind permission of the Patchwork and Quilting Guild.

The Publishers would like to thank the following: The Puncheon's Craft Studio, 73 High Street, Uckfield, East Sussex TN22 1AP, for their help and for preparing and supplying the slate frame on page 39 and the hoop shown on page 40; Ann Edwards, Mockrum, Bickington, Barnstaple, North Devon, EX31 2JG, for her help and for designing and supplying the handkerchief sachet on page 63 and the cushion on page 65.

ISBN 0 85532 669 7 (Pb)
ISBN 0 85532 676 X (Hb)

I wish to acknowledge the help I have been given in writing this book, especially Rosemary Allan, The Beamish Museum, Lesley Foster, Shipley Art Gallery and Alanna Knight.

Amy Emms, MBE.

Typeset by Genesis Typesetting, Rochester, Kent, England
Printed by Times Publishing Group

Contents

Introduction

The ancient craft of quilting is a decorative method of joining two or three layers of material together to provide warm clothing, bed covers or wall hangings. The word 'quilt' is believed to be derived from the Latin *'culcita'*, meaning a sack filled with feathers, wool or hair.

Long before it became a highly-prized craft, quilting was used for warm, sturdy garments and household furnishings but, like most old crafts, its early beginnings cannot be traced. It was known throughout the civilized world in ancient times, from China and India, to Persia, North Africa and Europe. In some early Egyptian friezes the garments suggest a primitive form of quilting, but this is mere guesswork. As with all needlecrafts, few examples have survived in reasonable condition but a Sicilian quilt, dating from circa 1400AD, is housed in the Victoria and Albert Museum in London.

In England and Wales during the Middle Ages soldiers wore a quilted garment with, or without, a covering of chain mail. This garment could be worn beneath a suit of armour to stop any chafing and also to give added protection against arrows and similar missiles. The outer layer could be of linen, canvas or even leather. During the Tudor dynasty, quilted garments became very fashionable and petticoats and doublets formed an essential part of feminine and masculine attire.

Quilting became almost an art form in England and Wales and reached the height of its glory during the reign of Queen Anne. It gradually declined in popularity, however, and had almost vanished by the nineteenth century but struggled to survive mainly in northern England and Wales, where traditional designs were handed down from mother to daughter.

The craft had been taken to North America by the early settlers in the seventeenth century and travelled west with them. By the nineteenth century it was so popular that gatherings at which women met regularly to quilt – much as Amy Emms remembers – became important social events and to this day, the craft has enjoyed almost unbroken popularity.

Quilting has four distinct forms; English or padded, corded or Italian, Trapunto or stuffed and shadow quilting. In a further method of simple flat quilting, two layers can be stitched together by means of an all-over decorative design. In English quilting the whole article is padded and the design is stitched over the entire area through three layers of fabric, forming the front, back and interlining. The bumps between the stitches form the patterns. In corded quilting, no interlining is used and the design is stitched to form a double outline through two layers of material, so that a cord can be inserted to form a relief pattern. Shadow quilting is similar to corded quilting but a thin, transparent fabric such as organdie is used for the top and the corded effect is achieved with brilliantly coloured wools which show through as soft, shadowy colours on the front. In Trapunto quilting two layers are used, one of top fabric and one of muslin. The design is first stitched, then areas of the muslin are padded from behind and, when completed, it is backed with a lining.

Simple, evenly-spaced running stitches are used for all of these methods to produce designs. Today, with the advent of sewing machine techniques, back stitch, zigzag and chain stitches are sometimes used, but this is not traditional quilting. Machines, moreover, cannot reproduce the soft, puffed outlines of hand quilting, or the satisfaction that comes from creating a family heirloom entirely by hand.

Both Amy Emms and her mother taught what was referred to as 'Durham' quilting but, in fact, County Durham covered quite a small area from the river Tees to the Tyne. Although the craft was practised throughout a much wider area of northern England, to help alleviate the particularly distressing poverty in County Durham, the Rural Industries Bureau and the Women's Institute did much to promote the craft as 'Durham' quilting and to find a market for the work in London. When the county boundaries were

***Opposite:** Olive Emms' wedding dress.*
This superb example of the craft of Durham quilting is
quilted and sewn together entirely by hand.

reorganised in 1971, the large towns of Gateshead, Sunderland and Washington were amalgamated to form part of the new county of Tyne and Wear and, nowadays, the craft is generally referred to as North Country quilting.

Quilting today can be used for bed covers, wall hangings, dressing gowns, evening jackets, cushions, nightdress cases, or for any item where padding is introduced either as a decorative feature, or for added warmth. Amy Emms has devoted her life to the craft of quilting and this book tells her fascinating story and gives instructions for working both the old and the new techniques. Examples of Amy's beautiful designs are also included, together with instructions for making cushions, full-sized quilts and garments.

Amy enjoying a cup of tea in her kitchen. The pot is kept warm with a quilted cosy.

Amy Emms' Story

I was born in 1904 in the little village of Fulwell, on the north-east coast of County Durham, near Sunderland. My father had died before I was born and with no pensions in those days, my mother had to work very hard to make a living and to bring me up. My only brother was fourteen when I was born and we lived in a small cottage, one of six houses in the row. We had candlelight and gas lamps but despite the lack of modern conveniences, it was a happy community of good neighbours, who seemed like one of the family.

My mother had to go out to work when I started school and when she came in after a hard day, she would start on a quilt which was always in the frame. These provided an additional source of income. I would sit and watch her and when I was seven I started threading the needles for her, see illustration 1. This was a great help, as the more I threaded, the more she used. She was a real country woman, carrying on the tradition of quilting which had been in her family for generations, and handed down from mother to daughter through the ages, see illustration 2.

When I reached fourteen, I began to sit down at the frame with her and found the craft very fascinating. I loved it, for while we both sat quilting mother would tell me about her early life and how they quilted at night because there was no entertainment, no television or radio. If people wanted entertainment, then they had to make their own. Since the quilts were worked by candlelight, I wondered how those earlier generations had managed to see the designs. Their method was to draw the pattern on to the fabric as they went along, using school chalk or the point of the needle, as the chalk rubbed off too easily.

When we were able to sit all day at the frame, the routine was that one of us would get up and make the meal while the other quilted uninterrupted. About the time I took up the craft, there was only one other woman in the area who quilted. Although she lived not far from us, she only took orders from a shop in the town, so I never saw any of her work.

At the time I was still threading needles, my mother decided to start a Quilting Club. You needed twenty people for this and very soon she had her list of names, all from the village. The next step was to put one-to-twenty numbers and the names on to separate pieces of paper. These were placed in a receptacle and on the night of the draw, two or three of the women would come to the house to see that it was carried out properly. One would draw a name, another a number, until a complete list was formed. The cost of a quilt was twenty shillings (£1.00p), but the first shilling was used to obtain the materials for the first quilt, so each Club member paid 21 shillings, (£1.05p). The first name and number had quilt No 1, the second No 2 and so forth.

When the Club was established it meant that my mother had to sit a full week to get the quilt completed and many times I have seen her sit up until the early hours of the morning to finish a piece of work in time. She kept on with the quilting club for a long time, until it happened that she could not manage to complete quilt No 20 by week 20.

By this time, I was able to help and we began making quilts for shops in the town. This was more profitable and as our work became known, we began to get orders from well-known people. The materials we used in those days were mainly plain Turkey red cotton on one side and a Paisley pattern on the other. The width of the materials was only 30in (76cm) and it took 18yd (16.50m) for a full-sized quilt measuring 90 by 108in (228 by 274cm).

In the 1920s we were able to buy sateens in beautiful colours and in widths of 30 and 36in (76 and 91cm). We chose contrasting colours for most of these quilts and the prices varied. From sateens, we went to silks and satins and, last of all, to nylon. We loved quilting with these materials as they were so much easier than the cotton type and we could purchase them in widths of 48 and 50in (122 and 127cm), which meant we only needed 12yd (11m) for a double bed sized quilt.

The padding, or 'wadding' as we called it, was cotton wool, either bleached to a pure white, or in an unbleached cream colour. Wadding had one draw-back; it contained small hard seeds and once the needle caught on one of those, inevitably a pricked finger followed. However, these old wadding quilts always washed like new and still do today.

I remember my mother going to the sales and buying remnants of material suitable for quilting. She cut these into strips and made what are known as 'strippy quilts'. The pieces left over from the quilts we had already made were cut into shapes and made up as patchwork quilts, or what we called 'everyday quilts'. All of these were quite heavy and a considerable weight to wash. Sometimes we made smaller sizes, suitable for the foot of the bed, called 'foot haps' in those days and now known as eiderdowns.

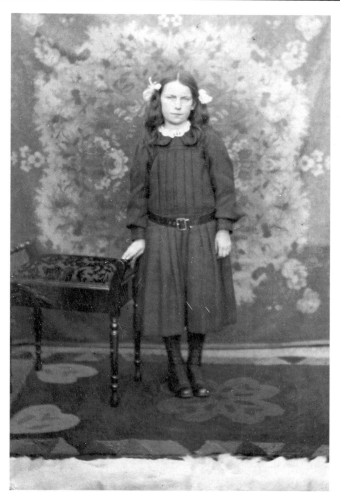

2. *My mother, aged 70 years.*

1. *Myself, aged 9 years.*

As the years went on the quality of my work improved. I discovered that I had a natural gift for quilting design and I began entering the Annual Shows in County Durham and Districts, where I won many prizes and certificates.

In 1914, the First World War broke out and our village school was taken over to billet the soldiers, so we were moved into the tiny chapel, or church. Sitting in hard pews was a lot different from desks and our lessons were restricted to four hours a day. They consisted mainly of sewing, or knitting mittens and helmets, known as 'balaclavas', for the soldiers. In those four terrible years of war, education was secondary and we lost a lot of valuable learning time.

When the war ended at last in 1918, I remember marching all round the town, so proud to be in the Peace Procession. I was fourteen. I left school then, as this was the statutory school leaving age, and went to a private Shorthand Academy, where I learned shorthand, typing and business training. After fifteen months I qualified, ready to take my first office job as a clerk in a garage. I was quite happy with this new experience and soon got used to office routine, working five-and-a-half days a week from 9am to 6pm on Mondays to Fridays and 9am to 2pm on Saturdays. Wages were very low in those days and the only amusements we had after work were dancing or going to the theatre, but for me most nights were spent at home, sewing or quilting. The village Church had a troop of Girl Guides and Sea Scouts, so I spent one night a week at the Church Hall.

In 1920, a friend introduced me to a boy named Albert. He was a glassmaker with a firm who made stained glass for cathedral and church windows. The firm is still in existence and their glass goes all over the world. It was fascinating to watch Albert working with pieces of coloured glass, shaping them into beautiful pictures and designs. We were married in 1924. My brother was in Canada, so instead of getting a home of our own, we stayed with my mother. This was very convenient as it meant that we could continue quilting together as we had done practically all my life, for we loved each other's company, sharing our memories and gossiping about the past.

In 1931 our son George was born. I remember the nurse saying on her last visit to me after the birth, 'I'll be back in five year's time'. I laughed, but it was true! In 1936 we were celebrating George's fifth birthday with a party for his friends and on the very next day a little daughter was born. George was coming home from school and a neighbour said to him, 'Hurry home, you have a little sister'. As he looked at the baby his little face lit up and he said, 'Mam, call her Olive'. This was the name of his favourite playmate and we decided that this should be our daughter's name too. Incidentally, the same nurse attended me for this birth. This time, when her visits ended four weeks later, she said 'I'll not be back any more. You

won't be needing me again'. And this prediction also came true!

We were still living in Fulwell in 1939 at the outbreak of the Second World War. Sunderland was a danger area, so arrangements were speedily made to evacuate all the children. George was eight and he left with about 200 other schoolchildren on Sunday morning, 8th September, to go by train to Yorkshire. The following morning I left with Olive, who was three, with about 40 other women who had children under school age. Some had babes in arms and we were a sorrowful sight carrying our luggage and gas masks and, as well as the all-important identity cards, we all had labels with our names pinned on to our coats.

We set off for Yorkshire at 7.30am and arrived in the late afternoon to be met by three billetting officers, all women. Finding places for all of us took quite some time, but we were mostly placed into good homes although this fact did little to cheer us up, feeling ourselves to be strangers among strange folk in a strange area. I was billeted with a young married couple who had a baby of nine months but at the end of two weeks I still couldn't settle down. I stayed for four months but I was still so homesick that I just wanted to take Olive back to Fulwell, so that's what I did.

I spent the New Year of 1940 in Fulwell on my own. My mother had a stroke that year and died within ten days, at the age of 78. My brother, who had returned from Canada still unmarried, kept the cottage on for a couple of years. Then, as a result of an accident going to work in the blackout, he also died in 1942. A sad end to my family.

In Yorkshire, the children of school age had to be billeted in another village six miles away, as there were no school facilities anywhere near their original location. As they reached school-leaving age they each had to return to their own home but George, and his mate Tommy, stayed on for the whole of the war. George had been very happy and well-cared for and his foster-parents wanted him to stay on with them permanently, since he was now like one of their own family. But we wanted him back home with us again. Even after all these years, I still keep in touch with my friends of the evacuation, who made me and mine so welcome in their homes.

Albert had been called up in 1941 for the Army. In May 1943 we lost our home in Fulwell and everything in it, as the result of a land-mine. We always took shelter in a cupboard under the stairs, since we felt safer there than in the air raid shelter outside in the yard. Rescued by the Air Raid Wardens, we were shocked and shaken but otherwise unhurt and more fortunate than most of our neighbours, some of whom were badly injured, but our little house with all its memories was completely demolished. We stayed with relatives until a friend rented us their small bungalow, which they had built some years

3. Albert, just before he retired from the glass works.

earlier for their invalid daughter. It was a lovely little home, built in a field but it contained everything we needed. We stayed there until winter set in, when we were given a council house at the west end of Sunderland, a new area for us where we would need to make new friends. However, it was something to have a roof over our heads, since there were some 200 homeless families in the area. The year 1943 had been

terrible for us. Albert had been discharged from the Army after two years' service, through ill health. He had been forced to take a light job, which he held until the war ended when the glass works, closed during the war years, was reopened. He remained at the glass works until 1967, when he retired, see illustration 3.

During the war, I had joined the Roker and Fulwell British Legion, where I became a Standard Bearer and a member of the Committee. When it became known that I was a quilter it wasn't long before I had twelve of the women members all eager to start on this fascinating 'hobby'. We arranged an afternoon meeting in the headquarters once a week. They began on cushion covers and did some very good work. Then one day we decided that it would be nice to sit as a 'quilting bee', and make a full-sized quilt to be raffled to raise funds. It took nearly a year to complete but we all enjoyed this joint effort. When we had finished the quilting and taken it out of the frame, ready to finish off the edges, a photographer who had heard about our quilt, arrived from the local newspaper. We were rather shy at the thought of being photographed at first, but were finally persuaded and a very good photograph it turned out to be, with the women sitting round the quilt as I watched them. We all treasured the original black-and-white photograph, see illustration 4, little realising that it would gain such honours as it has done up to this day. We now have copies in colour.

4. *Roker & Fulwell British Legion class,
showing our first completed quilt in 1945.*

Each year the British Legion holds an Annual Exhibition in June or July, so in the early 40s we also started entering our work in the Durham Quilting section, see illustration 5. For eight years running we gained top marks; 1st, 2nd and 3rd certificates, which brought us the Quilting Cup. After the eighth successive year, rumours went round that I was a professional quilter and it was felt that I should step down to let some of the other branches have a chance of winning. Had we continued for another two years, we would have been presented with the coveted Rose Bowl trophy. In our eight winning years I had often dreamed about the pleasure of receiving this personally at the annual prize-giving ceremony in the Durham City Town Hall. At this function, delegates

went up to the platform to receive the various Cups and as I attended the meeting one night, it came as a wonderful surprise when the Secretary and President of our branch presented me with a replica of the Quilting Cup, with the dates of our winning years inscribed on it.

The work in these exhibitions was really beautiful and quite exceptional. For some years, Lady Havelock-Allan performed the opening ceremony and as soon as she finished speaking, she always made a beeline for the quilting display and chatted to me about my craft. On one occasion a lovely white quilt which I had on display caught her eye. She loved it and begged me to sell it to her. Soon I was quilting for her personally. As a result of all these exhibitions, I was suddenly a local celebrity, with reporters and photographers wanting interviews.

One day in 1951 I was asked to go to the Education Office. I couldn't think what they wanted because both George and Olive had long since left school. I was somewhat taken aback when I was asked if I would like to teach quilting at evening classes. I had never done much teaching except at the British Legion, and 'handing down' my craft to my daughter in the time-honoured fashion, by teaching her when she was twelve how to make handkerchief cases. At this time there were two other evening class teachers in soft furnishings but only doing a little quilting, so I agreed to try.

My first class was at the Community Centre where I found 24 women all waiting patiently to begin. Some were quite young and one was over 70. First of all I talked to them, explaining about the craft and what they would need to bring the following week to enable them to start quilting, just the way I had been shown by my mother so long ago. Some made cushions, others chairback covers and sideboard runners, but all small items to begin with.

After the first year they had all done some beautiful work and I knew they were now quite capable of putting a quilt, or bedspread into the frame. Quilting frames were now being made in all sizes at the carpentry workshop in the Centre and some members had their own frames. We held the class in a very large room with trestle tables and chairs set all round the walls. There would be about 20 quilts in place and because they were too large to be taken home, they had to remain there covered up until the next quilting session. As the women entered the room they were like children at school, each knowing where their quilt was and going straight to it. Off came their coats and they sat down eagerly; while some put on their spectacles, others would be busy taking out scissors, thread and so forth. No time was wasted and they were all so friendly together, more like a family than members of an evening class. The two hours soon vanished, with the satisfaction of knowing that a little more work had been done and each quilt was two hours nearer completion. Most of the women were

5. *The British Legion exhibition of quilting
in Sunderland Town Hall in 1945. Cup winners again!*

6. *Part of the quilting class at the East Community Centre
in Sunderland, 1951.*

*7. Portrait of Mrs. Lough, who took me for my
City & Guilds Diplomas in 1952.*

very sorry they had to wait another week before they could continue, see illustration 6.

I had been teaching for more than a year when I was called back to the office. There I met some of the other evening class teachers. It so happened that there was no City & Guilds Diploma for quilting, so the organiser explained that to allow the classes to continue, those teachers without Certificates would have to step down. She advised me to go to Durham and take my Diplomas, so I applied to Durham Education Committee and was accepted. I was to go to college for two hours each week. I felt very strange that first Saturday morning when I went into the classroom and was told to sit down in a desk, a pupil

again after all those years. However, when my teacher, Mrs. Lough, saw my work she said she couldn't teach me anything, as I already knew as much as she did, see illustration 7.

I enjoyed those classes very much and I had no trouble getting my Diplomas, which were to prove a great help to me, especially in the new method of designing and finishing off the quilting with piping. I eventually began teaching women in Gateshead, as well as Durham, showing them how to draw the design with paper and pencil, before transferring it on to the material.

In 1953 I was asked to make a dressing gown for a French designer who came to visit me. She tried to explain what she required – in French! This was rather difficult for me to understand but when it was finished, reversible in blue and pink, she was delighted with the result. She kept it for many years and regularly reported that it was still as good as new. This achievement set me off making dressing gowns and I have made many since then, see illustration 8.

Meanwhile my children were growing up and making their own lives. My son, George, had joined the Merchant Navy in 1951 and was away at sea for five years. In 1955 he married and eventually had two

8. A quilted dressing gown made in 1953.

17

children, but in 1964 they went to live in Australia and have remained there, apart from a few visits home to see 'grandma'.

In 1957, my daughter Olive was to be married and she wanted a quilted wedding dress. Would it be heavy, she asked? What would it make afterwards? I suggested pram sets! We ordered white satin and found exactly the paper pattern we wanted. Soon I had it all designed and into the frame, ready to quilt. I was very eager to begin something which would give me such pleasure. How delighted we were when we finally took it out of the frame and began putting it together. It fitted perfectly, and Olive looked beautiful, see illustration 9. We also discovered that the circular skirt would make an ideal circular bed cover and the bodice would make a bed jacket. We had achieved so much on that day, and I was so thrilled that I had to shed a few tears.

The day of the wedding dawned and Olive's dress caused quite a sensation. It was greatly admired and that night the evening papers had a good write up about it, news having travelled fast. I received many letters as a result of this publicity and still keep a boxful to remind me of that lovely day. People wanted to join the classes, or to have private tuition. Picking out fifteen names and addresses, we soon had another two or three classes in progress.

Most unfortunately, the snow which had fallen thick and fast on Olive's wedding day, although very romantic for such an occasion, had made the hem of the dress wet and it was marked with the colour from the confetti and rose petals. Anyway, I regard my daughter's dress as one of my greatest achievements and the 'Wedding Gown' has been an attraction in exhibitions and museums all over the country ever since, see illustration 10. Perhaps one day we will send it to a museum but, at present, it is an heirloom and as a circular quilt looked lovely in their first home in Weardale. A few years later they moved to Yorkshire.

9. Olive outside the church, showing the train of her wedding dress.

10. *Olive in her wedding dress – one of my proudest moments.*

In 1959 we bought a little cottage in Weardale, ready for when Albert retired. For the next eight years we travelled there every weekend and at holidays, and I continued my quilting in both homes. We moved from Sunderland in March 1967 on Albert's 65th birthday, when he left his glass-making employment for the last time. We were sorry to leave behind all the happy years and the pleasant memories but we were eager, too, for our lovely little home in the country, see illustration 11.

Leaving our old home also meant that I had to retire from my evening classes. I was given a farewell party and a presentation, gifts from all of them, see illustration 12. I was also made an honorary member of the Community Centre and I decided that after such a full and active life, giving up the classes was going to be a nightmare for me. We were not long settled in our new life, however, when some of my old friends from the village where we now lived came to visit me and pressed me into joining the Women's Institute there. I promised I would, on the understanding that I was not going to take an active part. I just wanted to go along and enjoy their meetings. I was not there very long before they asked me to show examples of my craft at their Annual Show. These caused a great deal of excitement and I was asked if I would show some members how to quilt. I couldn't

refuse as I wanted the craft of Durham quilting to go on and never become a dying craft. So I agreed to show a few of them without a fee, if they paid for the use of the hall. They were delighted and soon I had a class of fifteen-to-twenty, which flourished for a number of years.

Soon after this class began, I was asked to give a quilting demonstration at the Women's Institute in the next village. I took along a lot of my equipment and we had a grand evening, talking about quilting and everything connected with it. After showing some of my work and a partly-finished dressing gown, which had just come out of the frame ready to put together, I happened to say, 'I like demonstrating but I'd rather be teaching'. Word soon got around and I was asked if I'd consider starting a class in their hall. I agreed, as before, as long as they paid for the hall. I continued teaching these two classes for some time, until I had so many demonstrations and exhibitions to attend that I couldn't continue any longer. Everyone was disappointed when the classes ended, especially as they were producing excellent work. Some of the members who had to leave the Dale kept in touch with me, however, and I was delighted to know that they had commenced classes in their new surroundings, as this was all part of keeping the craft alive.

12. *With all of my students at my retirement party from the East Community Centre.*

11. *A view of my cottage and, inset, the view from my sitting room.*

21

In 1971 my husband died very suddenly, after only four years of retirement. I could not let it become the end of my life and I made up my mind to go on quilting. It has always been a wonderfully fulfilling way of life; rewarding as a craft and I also think of it as an entertainment, providing very good company. It has always helped me a lot and been a comfort in sad times. Once quilting is in your blood, you want to go on and on and, as I tell my students, my motto is that a quilting frame has always been furniture in our house and as one article comes out, another goes in. We all have a gift of some kind, and mine is quilting.

I was asked to demonstrate quilting at the opening of the Beamish Open Air Museum in 1972, see illustration 13. That was a lovely day and I sat and talked, with my 'bits and pieces' in front of me and my frame and equipment, answering all the questions folks asked. The room was very old-fashioned and the building a piece of history. One little lad of about four stood in front of me and studied me very carefully before asking, 'Do you live here, missus?'. 'No, sonny, not here' I replied but everyone had a good laugh as he obviously thought the elderly lady sitting there with her quilting was a permanent part of the fittings! I was asked to go back again and have many times been allowed to borrow their beautiful quilts for exhibitions.

13. *Demonstrating quilting at the opening of the Beamish Open Air Museum in 1972.*

14a and b. The back and front view of the cope made for the Bishop of Derby in 1975.

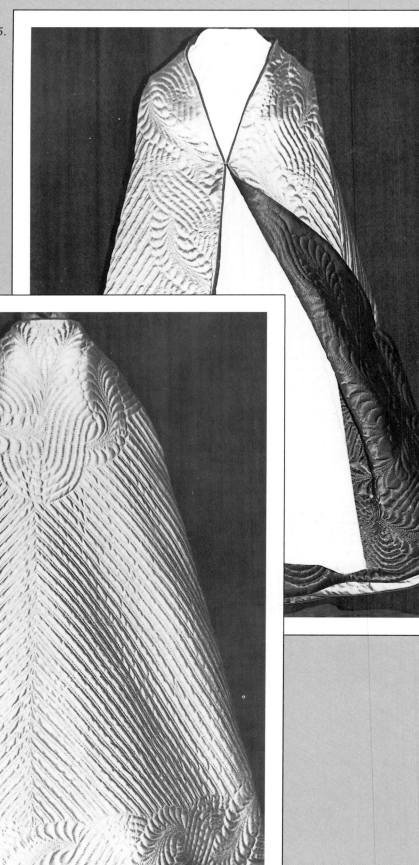

In my time I have made quilts for many titled ladies, including Lady Havelock-Allen, Lady Barnard, Lady Hesketh and Lady Scarborough. As well as my daughter's wedding dress, I also made a cope for a Bishop in 1975, see illustration 14 for the back and 14a for the front. I didn't know what a 'cope' was but I soon found out and the design was, appropriately, taken from a quilt I had on show in a cathedral at the time. The shape of the cope was a half-circle, taken from the skirt of the wedding gown and was coloured red on one side, with gold contrast. Over the years I have adapted the design of the cope in many different ways, as it is an extremely useful shape. A shortened version makes a beautiful bed cape, or a luxurious evening cape, which just covers the shoulders and keeps off any chill winds, see illustration 15.

15. An evening cape adapted from the cope.

16. *Demonstrating quilting for Shipley Art Gallery in 1978.*

At one of my classes, the Director of the Shipley Art Gallery in Gateshead came to see my students' work and asked me if I would demonstrate at his gallery, see illustration 16. Later I was asked to take classes there, or as they called it, a 'school'. I was very pleased to accept, as it meant one whole day's teaching on nine Saturdays in the year.

Opposite top: *general view of the Weardale valley.*

Opposite middle: *the river meanders through the field which runs along the bottom of my cottage. You can either cross it by the bridge, the ford or risk the stepping stones!*

Opposite bottom: *my cottage nestles in the background.*

The fame of my Durham quilting spread to films with the British Broadcasting Company, programmes with Tyne-Tees and Thames Television and to tapes for craft courses. The school at Shipley lasted for eight years and, very much against their wishes, I retired in March 1984, when the craft organiser was leaving to go into her own business of quilting. At that time I had students from all over Durham and Northumberland and as far away as York. Some of them now teach quilting and I hear from them regularly. In their letters they tell me that as well as teaching in schools, they have also been teaching in America and taking the craft to many other parts of the world. Through the years, members of the Craft Council have requested photographs for their books and magazine articles and my bookcase is now filled with quilting books.

I still continued quilting for pleasure and completed this wedding dress in 1979, see illustration 17, but one secret ambition I was to fulfil gave me great personal pleasure and that was being asked to make an altar cloth for my church in St. John's Chapel in January, 1979. The Vicar arranged for the material to be bought in London, red on one side, deep purple on the other. I pondered on what sort of pattern to use. Should it be, appropriately, Durham templates? Then I decided on a design from one of the church windows and the Vicar thought this was an excellent idea. It was such a pleasure to quilt and when it was completed with gold braid and fringing, it looked really lovely and the Vicar asked me if I would make the matching Fall, Book Marks and Service Cloth. These were dedicated one Sunday night in June, 1979, an occasion I found deeply touching.

Some time ago, when the Patchwork and Quilting Guild was formed, I received lots of mail from them

Opposite: a close-up picture of the train of Olive's wedding dress.

and arrangements were made for me to give a demonstration on quilting. Eventually a party of quilters and Guild members came to see me at Shipley Art Galleries, in Gateshead. Seeing me quilting, also seeing a film of me at work, they were well entertained and spent an excellent day, rounded off by asking me questions. After that, letter writing was kept up by each of us, exchanging our news, and this led to some letters being published in the Guild Magazine, or Newsletter. Very soon after this I was made an Honorary Member of the Guild. They forward me their quarterly magazines each year and I always look at them from cover to cover, as there is plenty of good news in them!

17. Ann Elliott's wedding dress, 1979.

Person with the
Leguin books
(ones we don't want)

Please fill in appropriate boxes for proper credit. Please list the item(s) returned and use the appropriate problem code and action code, as stated above.
You MUST list the TITLE CODE OR ISBN to receive proper credit.

DATE OF RETURN			YOUR CLAIM OR P.O. NUMBER		SHIP TO OR ACCOUNT NUMBER			
QTY ORDERED	QTY RECEIVED	QTY SHORT	QTY RETURNED	TITLE	TITLE CODE OR ISBN	LIST PRICE	DISCOUNT	PROBLEM CODE	ACTION CODE

Include the form in your return carton. Return the carton to the warehouse on the label. Affix our return label (located at the top right hand corne on the same side of this packing list) to the carton containing this form and indicate the number of cartons being returned. Returns must be Prepaid

18. The blue quilted wall hanging presented to Deirdre Amsden in 1982.

19. *Demonstrating quilting at the Minories, Colchester, in 1982.*

In 1982, I received news that the Secretary to the Guild, Deirdre Amsden, was retiring from the post after quite a few years of service and everybody was sorry to lose her. They asked me if I would make a wall hanging as a gift for her but it must be kept a secret, as they did not want her to hear about it. Materials were sent to me and before I had it completed, another letter arrived inviting me to their Annual General Meeting. This was to be held in May and they asked if I would present the wall hanging to Deirdre at the meeting. I travelled to Birmingham on the day with the Organizer of Crafts from the Shipley Art Galleries. We were made so welcome by everyone and received 'VIP' treatment from the moment of leaving to returning home. During the afternoon I presented Deirdre with her parting gift and she was really taken aback, as she never guessed anything about it. She was so thrilled, saying she couldn't thank me as she was lost for words! When I receive letters from her the wall hanging is always mentioned, see illustration 18.

After the meeting at Birmingham, I went to Colchester with the Guild and demonstrated one

afternoon at the Minories, see illustration 19. It was another good exhibition of quilts and a chance to meet new quilters. We were always made very welcome and it was a pleasure to be among so many enthusiasts.

As the years went by, many university students going in for Domestic Science wanted to take Durham quilting, (or North Country quilting as it became), as one of their subjects. They would write to me, asking if they could come and visit me and would I kindly help them. Well, I could not refuse and always had to say, 'Yes'. Some would come and spend all day, taking photographs and making tape recordings, as they said these helped them a lot. Some even brought their parents with them and we all spent hours talking about the craft. As each one received their Finals, they always let me know the result. These were excellent and photographs of their quilting always seemed to receive extra good marks. I must have taught dozens of students in my time and I felt these results were a great honour, not only to the students and myself but to the craft.

31

On a never-to-be-forgotten day in November, 1983, I received a letter marked 'OHMS', sent from the Prime Minister in Downing Street. It was to inform me, in confidence, that she had in mind to appoint me, on the occasion of the forthcoming list of New Year's Honours, as a Member of the Order of the British Empire, subject to approval. My eyes filled with tears of joy at this wonderful surprise.

From then until the end of December, I waited patiently for the news to arrive. The first call on the morning of January 1st, 1984, was from Tyne-Tees Television, congratulating me on my Award. The 'phone never stopped ringing for the rest of the day and by night time, it was red hot! Congratulations came from far and wide and I was overcome at the honour.

On January 12th, 1984, a letter arrived asking me to attend the Investiture to be held at Buckingham Palace on Tuesday the 21st February, 1984. My daughter and son-in-law were permitted to accompany me as guests to watch the ceremony. We soon made all the necessary arrangements for travelling to London on the Monday morning, to enable us to settle down and be ready for Tuesday morning, arriving at the Palace before ten o'clock.

The great day arrived and we had a lovely ride through London, before reaching The Mall. Driving up this wide avenue it seemed that every other car was going to the same place as we were. The passengers were mostly men in top hats and tails and ladies, beautifully gowned in rainbow colours. Reaching the Palace gates we had to wait for a while, among a huge crowd. Lots of photographers were there, all asking to take photographs, see illustration 20. As soon as the gates opened we walked into the grounds and made for the main entrance. Once inside, it was like a fairy tale come true! We were then shown to the cloak rooms, recipients to the right and guests to the left, and from there we were escorted to the Reception Hall. This was truly magnificent. Here I waited along with another 149 men and women. I had the company of a lady from Ireland who, like myself, was a bit puzzled as to what we had to do next. We soon received instructions, however, which were very simple and nothing to worry about. I learned later that twelve men were Knighted at this Investiture and 150 men and women received the OBE, while another 150 received the MBE.

We were then taken from the Reception Hall and escorted to the Ballroom, where the Investiture takes place. This room is too beautiful to describe in my simple words. Seeing the Queen standing there, so graceful and smiling as she pinned the Award to each coat, made such a lovely picture and one I shall always treasure. What with Her Majesty's handshake, her warm smile and the few words she spoke to me, I was overcome with emotion and had such a lump in my throat I couldn't swallow. The ceremony finished about 12.30pm and as we were leaving the Palace, we had a quick look round. There were men in uniform everywhere, all so smart you couldn't tell if they were statues or real men! It was a wonderful day and an experience I shall never forget.

Ever since receiving that letter in November I have wondered, also tried to find out, who sponsored me for this great honour. Up to this day I have never succeeded but now I have an opportunity of saying thank you from the bottom of my heart to the person,

21. My treasured medal.

20. *Taken at Buckingham Palace with my MBE award in 1984.*

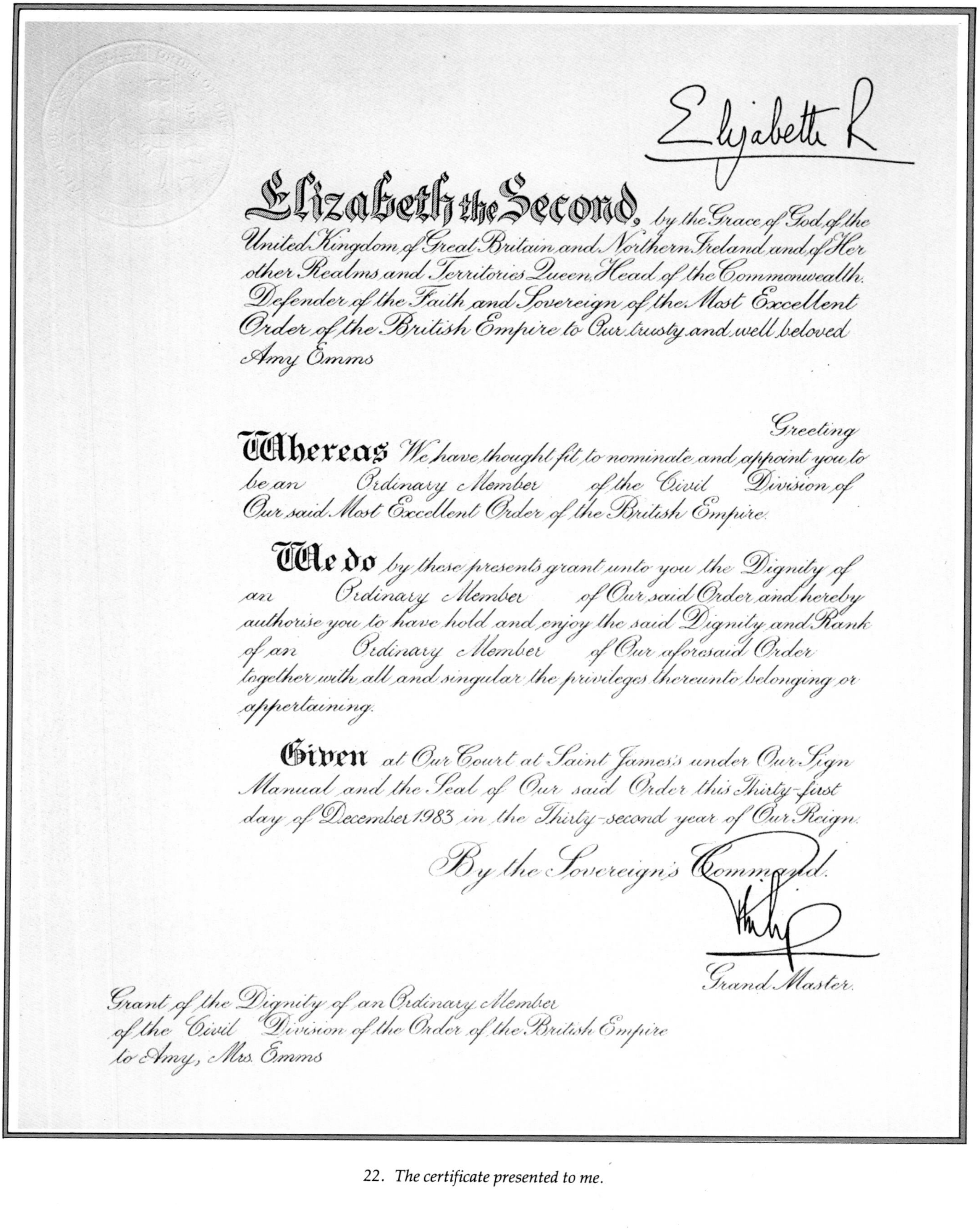

Elizabeth R

Elizabeth the Second, by the Grace of God, of the United Kingdom of Great Britain and Northern Ireland and of Her other Realms and Territories Queen, Head of the Commonwealth, Defender of the Faith and Sovereign of the Most Excellent Order of the British Empire to Our trusty and well beloved

Amy Emms

Greeting

Whereas We have thought fit to nominate and appoint you to be an Ordinary Member of the Civil Division of Our said Most Excellent Order of the British Empire.

We do by these presents grant unto you the Dignity of an Ordinary Member of Our said Order and hereby authorise you to have hold and enjoy the said Dignity and Rank of an Ordinary Member of Our aforesaid Order together with all and singular the privileges thereunto belonging or appertaining.

Given at Our Court at Saint James's under Our Sign Manual and the Seal of Our said Order this Thirty-first day of December 1983 in the Thirty-second year of Our Reign.

By the Sovereign's Command.

Grand Master.

Grant of the Dignity of an Ordinary Member of the Civil Division of the Order of the British Empire to Amy, Mrs. Emms

22. *The certificate presented to me.*

34

23. *Working on a quilt for Lord Hesketh in 1982.*

or persons responsible. It means such a lot to me and when I wear my medal on very special occasions, see illustration 21, I am filled with pride. The Certificate of Honour, received later from London, is framed for all to see and admire, see illustration 22.

To bring my story up to date, in 1982 I completed a quilt for Lord Hesketh, see illustration 23. In 1986 I had work on exhibition in Canterbury Cathedral and in 1987 I was asked to make a quilt for the Liberty's of London Exhibition. This last item was a great treat and a pleasure to work on and see the patterns forming. I always keep count of my time spent quilting and this one took 450 hours in all. It was a great thrill to be invited to the opening of the Exhibition on October 14th, 1987 and there were 200 quilts on display – it was a wonderful sight. My own quilt in cream Chinese silk was displayed on a bed at the entrance to the exhibition and I felt very proud indeed, especially when the press wanted pictures for magazines and newspapers. Next day I demonstrated my quilting in Liberty's magnificent shop and I was delighted to have a 'Durham quilt' for sale at the end of the exhibition! It was a great pleasure to speak to quilters from all over the world, as well as a lot of my good friends over many years, who are also members of the Patchwork and Quilting Guild.

Today I am still actively engaged in exhibiting my own work, and in judging other examples. It is so rewarding to see the current world-wide interest in the craft and the very high standard of quilting which is being achieved. I also take part in television programmes, or give talks about quilting, when requested. The materials and methods may have altered but I still prefer to stick to the old ways and I am doing all I can to promote a love for the craft that has filled my life.

People sometimes ask me if I feel sorry to part with a quilt, after all the work I have put into it. I can only say that I hope the pleasure the quilt gives to the receiver is equal to the pleasure I have had in making it. My only regret is that I didn't keep count of everything I have made in my time and the hours I have spent quilting. For a long time I couldn't have told you how long it took me to make a quilt, as I never kept a note of the hours. For years now, however, I have kept a record of the time spent at the frame each day. I jot down on my frame the time I begin and end and at the end of the day, I total the hours and enter them in a small notebook. It usually takes from 270 to 300 hours to complete the quilting and about one week to put it together and complete it. Although putting a new quilt into the frame is a delight, an even greater pleasure is taking it out and feeling that this is another achievement – well done!

Finally, it is my hope that everyone who reads my book will enjoy it as much as I have enjoyed writing it, and will discover how much pleasure is to be derived from this beautiful craft. Once quilting gets into your blood, you will want to go on and on. As I tell my students, the more you do the better quilter you will become, as you constantly learn by your mistakes. I think you'll agree that I'm living proof of the adage, 'You're never too old to learn'.

The craft of
Durham quilting

Tools and materials used in Durham quilting

Before you start to quilt, you must make sure that you have all the bits and pieces you need to hand. A quilting frame is essential but the fabric is really a matter of personal choice and what pleases you, although it must suit the purpose for which it is intended. You can easily begin to experiment with cheap remnants until you feel you can handle something a bit more special.

Quilting frames or hoops

You can't quilt unless you keep the three layers firmly together and under a certain amount of tension. You must either buy, or get a local handyman to make a frame. The frame can be up to 9ft (2.75m) long for something as big as a full-sized quilt and as you probably wouldn't be able to buy one this size, it would have to be specially made for you. A 3ft (91cm) frame for smaller items can easily be made, or it would not be too expensive to buy.

The modern quilting hoop is a form of embroidery hoop. They have some advantages over a frame for small items, as they can be carried around and it is also possible to quilt sitting comfortably in an armchair. Such luxury was unheard of in my day and this is not the traditional method! I, personally, always use a frame as do all my students.

Traditional quilting frames

In the early days these would be made individually to fit the size of each quilt by a male relative or local carpenter, see Fig 1. This type can be copied today and made from hard or soft wood. When completed, however, it needs to be carefully rubbed down with sandpaper, to stop the fabric catching on it.

To make a large frame suitable for a full-sized quilt, the two long ends, or rails, see (a) on Fig 1, need to be about 8 to 9ft (2.44 to 2.75m) long. Where these come into contact with the quilting fabric, they can be covered with soft, cotton cloth lightly nailed in place underneath, but this is not essential. They are made from square, or rectangular pieces of timber, thick enough to allow for slots to be cut into each end. Ask the carpenter to make sure that the finished length of each rail is sufficient to include space for the webbing and the slots for the stretchers. Extra at each end must also be allowed so that the frame can be

fig 1 traditional quilting frame

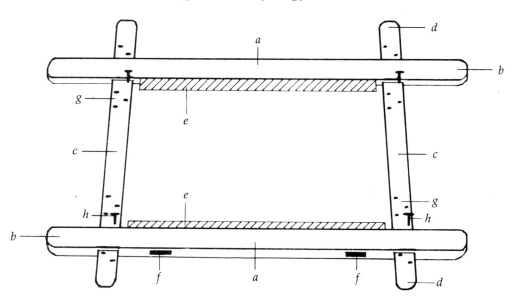

supported on sturdy tables, or chests of drawers at each end, see (b).

The two short ends, or stretchers, see (c) are used to tighten up the layers of fabric. They are made from thinner timber than the rails and are shorter, about 39in (1m). It helps if the top and bottom ends are rounded off, so they can easily be slotted into the rails, see (d).

Pieces of strong webbing must be secured with brass tacks along the length of the inner edge of each rail, between the slots, see (e), so that the lining material can be stitched in place.

You can quilt smaller items on a large frame by cutting another set of stretcher slots inside the outer sets, see (f). In this case, the webbing must be replaced to come between the new set of slots.

Two rows of holes are drilled into each stretcher, about ¾ to 1in (2 to 2.5cm) apart, to take the pegs which hold the frame in place, see (g). The old pegs were made of roughly-fashioned wood, with a knob at the top and a tapered shank, see (h).

Ready-made quilting frames

You can buy these today with, or without, stands, see Fig 2. They come in a variety of small sizes but it is a job to find one to fit a full-sized quilt as most stockists do not have room to store them. The version shown here illustrates how a small piece of quilting can be set into a large frame. Stitch a firm piece of calico into the frame as a backing and pin, then tack the quilting lining, wadding and fabric on top of this. Tape the backing to the side edges. *Before* beginning to quilt, secure the edges of the quilting layers to the backing and from *behind* cut out the centre section of the backing, otherwise you will be stitching through the calico.

One improvement over the traditional slate frame is that some models have a pivoting top, so that the work can be tilted towards the quilter, but this is a matter of personal choice. The finish is also superior to a home-made model, with rounded nail heads and some even have a rolling mechanism to tighten up the fabric.

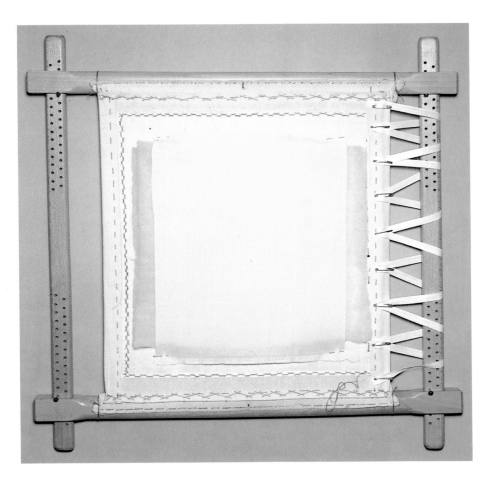

fig 2 ready-made quilting frame

39

When buying a frame, visit a specialist stockist where you can see a good selection of different models and find one to suit your purpose.

Quilting hoops

When using these hoops, the lining fabric is secured and kept at the correct tension by a butterfly-type screw fitted on to the outer edge of the hoop. These hoops are small, lightweight and portable and come in a variety of sizes, from 10in (25cm) to 23in (58cm) diameter, see Fig 3. It will help to keep the lining secure if you first bind the inner hoop – something like a 1in (2.5cm) bandage is ideal. The wadding and top fabric are then pinned and tacked in place on top of the lining but are not secured in the hoop.

Some models are available with a stand which allows the angle of the hoop to be adjusted, but these are not really satisfactory as the hoop tends to form an oval-shape, which affects the tension of the fabric and pulls it out of shape.

fig 3 quilting hoop

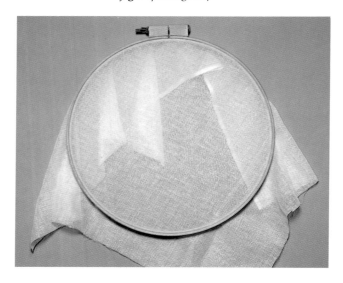

Fabrics

Each Durham quilted design consists of three pieces of fabric; the top layer, the middle layer of wadding and the bottom layer, or lining. You must give a great deal of thought to the right choice of fabric, particularly for the top and lining. For instance, if you are making a full-sized quilt you must first decide whether it is to be reversible, in which case you will need fabrics of similar qualities on both sides. If only one side of a design is to be viewed, however, such as with a wall hanging, a cheaper fabric can be used for the lining. When making a garment, such as a baby jacket, the underside can be of muslin, as the finished item will be lined in the ordinary way.

Colour must also play a part in the choice of fabric,

especially if the quilting is needed for a particular room-setting. You must also decide whether the item is to be washed or dry-cleaned and ensure that the fabric is suitable for these methods, as well as being colour-fast. It doesn't pay to rush into your first piece of quilting, as all your enjoyment can be wasted if you don't give enough thought to these points.

Natural fibres

The quilter today has many more fabrics available than we did in the early days. Natural ones, such as cotton, are still the most popular as they are hard-wearing and easy to quilt. Glazed furnishing cotton is very good but suitable linen is hard to find. Pure silk and satin are very luxurious and lovely to work on but need delicate handling and after-care and are also expensive. Most wool fabrics have too open a weave to quilt easily and can add a great deal of weight to a design. A stretchy knitted type of fabric should not be used as it will pucker and it can also cause unsightly, bulky seams.

Man-made fibres

Man-made materials and mixtures of synthetic and natural fibres are widely available. These are hard-wearing, launder well and are usually easy to handle. However, some pure synthetic fibres are not as pliable as natural fabrics and some are too slippery, making quilting very difficult.

Mixtures of polyester and cotton are very good but make sure that the polyester content is less than the cotton. The material must be thick enough not to allow the thread and seams to show through.

Wadding

The middle layer of the quilt is made of wadding, or 'batting' as it is called in America, and it serves two purposes. Firstly, it adds warmth to the quilted item and secondly, it causes the pattern to puff up into 'blisters' between the outline rows of stitching.

Until about the middle of the 1940s wadding was always made of natural fibres; wool in the very earliest history of quilting and cotton from the early part of the nineteenth century. Most quilters still prefer a cotton wadding, which is bought by weight in rolls. When the packet is opened the wadding needs to be unfolded and left in a warm place, such as the airing cupboard, to expand. Wool and cotton wadding must be quilted with very fine stitches to ensure that the fibres do not cling together when washed, making the quilting go lumpy.

With the introduction of man-made fibres, quilters now have a wider choice of wadding. Some qualities are rather harsh and difficult to quilt but one of the most popular ones is made from polyester fibres. This comes in different widths suitable for anything from tiny baby garments to full-sized quilts and is inexpensive, lightweight and easy to launder. It is also available in full bed-size widths.

Make sure that the wadding is bonded and that the layers do not part easily. If it isn't bonded together, fibres may pull through to the surface of the quilting with the thread and spoil the appearance of your design. Do not wash or iron wadding before you begin to quilt and once a quilt is completed it should not be pressed.

If you cannot obtain wadding in the full width you require, one section can easily be joined to another by butting the edges together but *not* overlapping them, and then sewing them together with herringbone stitch, see Fig 4. Keep the two edges straight.

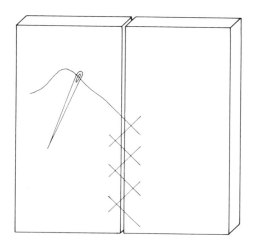

fig 4 joining two pieces of wadding together with herringbone stitch

Thread

The sort of thread you use depends on the type of fabric you are quilting but it must be strong enough to withstand constant use and laundering, or cleaning. Any breaks in the stitching will ruin the outlines of a design and also allow the wadding to shift about. As a general rule of thumb, I feel it is best to use unmercerised cotton thread with cotton fabrics, silk thread with silk fabrics and a cotton-covered synthetic thread with man-made fibres.

Specialist quilting suppliers can now provide a variety of suitable threads in a wide range of colours. If you are in any doubt, however, it is best to use a No 40 cotton thread. Interesting results can be achieved by using a thread which contrasts with the fabric, see the cushion shown on page 65.

Needles

These should be short and firm, with a small eye and are referred to as 'betweens'. The sizes vary from No 7 to No 10, depending on the type of thread being used. Sizes 7 and 8 are the largest, both in thickness

and length. Sizes 9 and 10 are the smallest and also help to keep your quilting stitches short.

I usually use a No 8 as these needles are just the right length for me for sewing with a thimble. They will not bend or break easily with the constant rocking movement needed to produce a neat line of quilting stitches.

Design markers

To transfer your design on to the fabric, a suitable type of marker must be used. This should give a clear line to follow which must be removable, or invisible, when the work is finished. I find it is impossible to recommend a marker which suits all purposes but the following list will help you to decide.

Chinagraph pencils: these leave a very clear quilting line and are available in different colours. The lines are very difficult to remove, however, and it takes two or three washes before they disappear.

Cobbler's awl: I have used all kinds of tools for marking but find this method is the best, as the wooden handle of the tool gives a good grip. Do not use the exact point of the awl or you will cut into the fabric. Hold the awl in your working hand and press the fabric down with your other hand, then use the side of the point to trace the design, going over the lines a few times. If you are using tracing paper, this will be cut but the fabric will be very clearly marked.

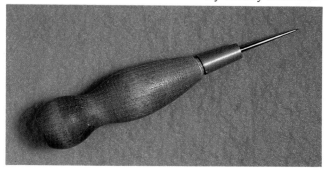

This is the cobbler's awl I use to mark out my designs.

Coloured pencils: use a pencil of a slightly darker shade of the colour of the fabric and draw the lines very lightly. They will disappear when the quilting is completed, as they will be hidden by the stitches. A water-soluble coloured pencil leaves a clearly visible line, but this can be lightly sponged away with clean water when the work is finished, taking care not to make the fabric too wet.

Dressmaker's chalk: this is the old traditional method but the chalk is now available in pencil form. The marks rub off very easily, however, so this method is not really suitable when a design has to be drawn on the fabric before being put into the frame, or for hoop quilting.

Dressmaker's carbon paper: this is useful if you are transferring a paper pattern, such as diamond filling, on to the fabric. Pin the pattern on top of the carbon and place the paper with the carbon side down over the fabric. Trace the lines with a pencil, or tracing wheel. The lines will only disappear with washing, or cleaning.

Needle marking: scoring the design on to the fabric with a needle is another traditional method. Use a thick needle with a large eye which is threaded with a short length of yarn, as this makes it easier to hold. Hold the needle level with the surface of the fabric, press it down and draw round the template. This is only suitable for natural fibres, however, where the impression will remain long enough to complete the quilting.

Templates

When you begin to plan a design you will need an outline of each motif you intend to use, such as a rose, or straight feather, see page 90. These outlines are referred to as 'templates' and can be purchased ready-made from specialist shops, or made from cardboard, thin plywood, firm plastic or even strong brown paper. The way in which these motifs are placed, together with infill and border patterns, forms the design of a quilt.

Ready-made templates

These are usually made of clear, rigid plastic, similar to a stencil, with any necessary filling-in lines of the motif cut out, ready to draw in place on the fabric.

Home-made templates

These are much more basic and usually just give the outline of the motif, so any additional filling in needs to be drawn freehand. To make your own accurate template, place a piece of clear, thin plastic over the motif you have chosen and trace the design on to it with a pencil. Find the centre of the motif as this will mark the first cut. Now mark all the various slits in the design, allowing for small joins between each one, or the template will fall apart. Use a small, sharp craft knife and carefully cut out the slits, remembering to allow enough space to take the tip of your marking tool.

The motifs given in this book, see page 88, can be enlarged or reduced to the size you require, then cut out and mounted on card. To adjust the size to suit your purpose either take a photograph in black-and-white and send the negative away to have a print enlarged or reduced, or use a photocopier to enlarge or reduce the size, although this method is not so exact. You can also obtain a device called a pantograph from most art or craft shops, see page 58.

Thimbles

It is absolutely vital to use a strong thimble on the middle finger of the hand used for sewing, usually the right hand. This finger controls the needle, pushing it through the three layers of material and it is used to produce the 'rocking' motion needed to make a line of several running stitches together. Some quilters also wear a thimble, or protector, on the finger of the other hand which is used to feel the needle coming through the fabric, usually the forefinger of the left hand, as well as on the thumb of the hand used for sewing.

Fingers and thumbs become very sore with the pricking of the needle and if some protection is not worn, your fabric can become stained with little spots of blood. As soon as you see one of these, rub it with a little of your own spittle, before it soaks in. It may help to harden your fingers by rubbing them with surgical spirit. If you are a really keen quilter you will prick your forefinger with every stitch as you feel for the needle point under the work, and the thumb of your working hand as you guide the needle through to the front again!

Other items

You will probably have most of the bits and pieces you need to hand.

Greaseproof paper: this is used for ruling up filling in patterns, such as diamonds, when a template is not needed, see page 88.

Pins: use dressmaker's pins to secure the filling in drawing to the fabric and safety pins to secure the tape at the sides of the frame.

Rules: a strong ruler, showing both Imperial and metric measurements is needed for drawing filling in patterns. When working any of the designs given in this book, use either Imperial or metric measurements but do not mix them, as the two systems are not inter-changeable.

Scissors: you need a large pair, sharp enough to cut through all three layers of quilting, and a small pair for snipping the threads.

Tape: narrow ½in (1cm) tape is needed to lace the fabric to the frame.

Begin with a quilted cushion

Now you are ready to learn the new method of the art of quilting. Rather than just fiddling with oddments of material, start with something useful and what better than a small cushion! You begin the stitching on the back, using diamond filling, so that when you come to work on the front, your stitching will have improved with practice. Also, when you have completed this project, you will find you have the confidence to make something more ambitious.

Size

To fit a cushion 20in (51cm) square

Materials

1yd (1m) of 44in (112cm) wide fabric for top and piping
¾yd (69cm) of 44in (112cm) wide fine cotton for the lining
Packet of nylon wadding, 2oz (50g) weight
2¼yd (2m) fine piping cord
Thread to match
Packet of No 8 betweens needles
3 buttons
Greaseproof paper

Cutting method

Cut 2 pieces of greaseproof paper 20 × 20in (51 × 51cm)
Cut 1 piece of material for top of cushion 22 × 44in (56 × 112cm)
Cut 1 piece of lining 22 × 44in (56 × 112cm)

Step 1: preparing the design

Take one piece of the greaseproof paper and use this for the back of the cushion. Fold crossways twice from corners to corners. This will give you the exact centre of your cushion. Now take a pencil and ruler and place the ruler on the paper, exactly on the crease and draw a line down both sides of the ruler from corner to corner. Lift the ruler and draw another line the same width from the first line. Continue until all the paper is covered, then do the same from the other two corners, each side of the ruler as before. These lines form equally-shaped spaces, called 'diamonds' and are used for filling in between patterns, see Fig 1.

Now take the second piece of paper and use this for the front of the cushion. Draw a line all round the outer edges, about 1in (2.5cm) in. This is for the

piping cord. Crease the paper from corners to corners as for the back, marking the centre. Decide on your design and choose only one, or two, templates, which are quite sufficient for a cushion. If a feather is your choice, place the template on one of the creases and draw all round it, then remove it and draw it on the other three creases. Then fill in the feather lines by freehand, or by placing the pattern beneath the greaseproof paper and following the lines shown on the feather. Make sure you also draw two lines down the centre of the feather, about ¼in (6mm) apart. By working freehand, you will begin to enjoy designing your own patterns. Fill in the remaining blank spaces with diamonds, going from corner to corner to the centre. As an alternative, a rose pattern in the centre and a small cable pattern round the edge looks nice, or even a template placed in between the crossed lines makes a good design, see Fig 2.

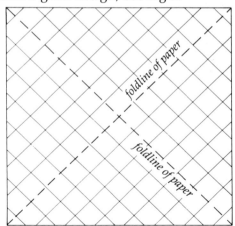

fig 1 cushion back
marking diamond infill pattern on greaseproof paper

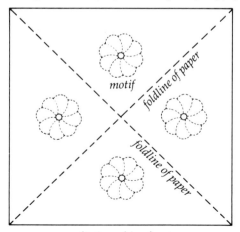

fig 2 cushion front
marking motifs on greaseproof paper

fig 1 *transferring the design on to the fabric*

Step 2: transferring the design

Cut your cushion material to give the full size of 22 × 44in (56 × 112cm) and mark a straight line across the centre, either with tacking thread or a chalk mark. This is then cut into two equal pieces when it is quilted, one for the back and one for the front of the cushion.

Next, fold a tablecloth or sheet into four thicknesses and lay this flat on a table as padding. Place your material on top, right side up, and pin it round the edges to the padding, about 2in (5cm) apart. Place the patterned greaseproof paper on top of the material, leaving 1in (2.5cm) clear all round the edges of the material, as each piece of the material is 22in (56cm) square and the paper is only 20in (51cm) square. Pin the paper every 2in (5cm) apart right through both paper and material to the padding. This will keep it firm all the time you are transferring the design. Begin with the diamond side first. When making up the cushion, keep the pencil marks top-side up, otherwise the lead pencil mark will be visible on the material.

Now transfer the pattern on to the material by placing a ruler on top of the greaseproof paper near the first mark, press down with your left, or non-working hand, and with a cobbler's awl, or the tool of your choice, rule lines from corner to corner in both directions. Do not use the point of the awl or you will cut your material. Using the side, the paper will be torn but not the fabric.

For the front of the cushion, you cannot use a ruler for the feathers or rose pattern, or template of your choice, as the ruler is only for straight lines. Instead, press the template down with your fingertips, going slowly round the design with the awl. If you press down very hard you will see the transferred design plainly on the material but you need to go over the design a few times to get the best results. To enable the design to be seen more clearly in the photograph, I am using dressmaker's chalk to fill in the design, see Fig 1.

Step 3: preparing the frame

The design is now ready to place in the frame. First of all, turn in the edges of the lining about ¼in (6mm) and pin it to the webbing on each rail of the frame. Now sew it in place along each edge, making sure you put a few stitches one on top of the other at the start and finish, as when you begin to quilt you have to give a little pull as you work, which could detach the lining from the frame if it isn't secured. Use hemming stitch to sew over the top of the lining and the webbing on both rails. As you go, make sure it is pinned in straight, or else it will gather up, see Fig 1.

When the lining is sewn into the frame, take the rail from the far side and turn the fabric round and round the rail, until about 18in (46cm) is left, (or about arm's length), see Fig 2, put the stretchers in place, see Fig 3, and peg into place, see Fig 4. Do not have it too taut, or you will not manage to pick up the bottom lining when you are quilting.

Cut the wadding the same size as your top material, joining if necessary to give 22 × 44in (56 × 112cm), and place it on top of the lining, nice and straight, see Fig 5.

Lay the top material on top of this, see Fig 6, and on the edge pin, then tack along the three layers. This helps to keep the layers firm when quilting, see Fig 7.

Smooth the wadding and material to the far edge, letting the loose part hang over the frame. Pin along the far edge of the wadding and top fabric *only*, nice and firm, about every 2in (5cm), see Fig 8. Always watch these pins when you are quilting, as the work is taken up as you quilt and the pins may cut into the fabric. So every time you turn your work, check the pins.

Now tape the side edges of your work over the stretchers, to keep these firm and straight, see Fig 9. Use ½in (1cm) wide tape, not bias binding, and allow four times the length of the stretcher for each side. Lightly tack the three layers of the quilt together to hold them in place, working in a grid of about 3in (7.5cm) and starting in the centre each time. Begin with a half bow in the tape at the top of one of the stretchers and take the tape across to the quilt, make a 'v' shape in the tape and secure the fold in place with a safety pin. Take the tape across the top of the stretcher, then underneath and across to the quilt again, make a 'v' shape and secure the fold in place with a safety pin. Continue in this way to the end of the stretcher and tie the tape in another bow to fasten. Repeat along the other edge. As you quilt, remember that you will need to let the lacing out again, as you are taking up some of the tension.

fig 1 attaching the lining to the rails of the frame

45

fig 2 *(top left)*
turning the fabric round the far side rail

fig 3 *(bottom left)*
putting in the side stretchers

fig 4 *(top right)*
putting in the pegs

fig 5 *(bottom right)*
placing the wadding on top of the lining

fig 6 (top left)
placing the marked fabric on top of the wadding
this shows the front of the cushion

fig 7 (bottom left)
tacking the wadding and top fabric along the bottom edge

fig 8 (top right)
pinning along the far edge

fig 9 (bottom right)
taping the side edges to the stretchers

fig 1 showing the position of the hands when beginning to quilt

Step 4: beginning to quilt

Make sure you are sitting comfortably, relax and don't worry! Have a few needles ready threaded, as this is easier than stopping to thread them while working. Use No 8 betweens and an 18in (46cm) length of thread. You are using running stitch throughout. Knot the end of the thread with a single knot. With your left, or non-working hand, underneath and your right, or working hand, on top, see Fig 1, insert the needle about 1in (2.5cm) away from your first line just into the top material and part of the wadding, then return it to the top again, see Fig 2. Now pull the knot through so that it is caught in the wadding, see Fig 3. All knots and ends must be lost in the wadding in this way, as both sides must be alike with no knots showing.

Make a small back stitch, as this stops the stitches from pulling out. The needle is now between your finger and thumb and must go through the three layers. Start with two or three running stitches and

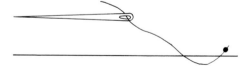

fig 2 knot lying on the surface wadding

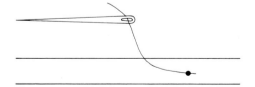

fig 3 knot pulled through and caught in wadding

fig 4 beginning to quilt, this shows the front of the cushion

remember, if you prick your fingers both underneath and on top, you have two more when the first ones get sore! Draw the thread up and give a little pull, not too hard or you will make a wavy line and the stitches will be lost in the wadding and not laid on top of your work, see Fig 4. After you get into the rhythm try and get more stitches on the needle. You are quilting diamonds, so work up the first line to about 8 or 10in (20 or 25.5cm), just as much as will run in, say, once or twice over your nearside rail. When you have got this far, turn with a back stitch and come down to the edge again, then another back stitch before going up the next line. You are quilting 'tent' shapes.

When that line is complete, go back and start the second line and when crossing a quilted line, just use an ordinary stitch through it, then continue with running stitch again. When coming to the end of the thread, or the end of a row, work a back stitch then take the needle up about 1in (2.5cm) away from the line, between the two top layers, pull the thread through and cut it off, letting it disappear in the wadding. Begin with a new thread and off we go again, stitching as before. Always work from front to back and from right to left, unless you are left-handed then, of course you will go the opposite way.

It is so fascinating to see the patterns form and most interesting going from one to the next. Always use infill patterns to cover the background of your quilting, and between motifs, so that the wadding is held firmly in place. As a general rule, no more than 2in (5cm) square should be left unquilted.

After working as much quilting as will turn under once or twice on the rail, remove the tapes and pull out the stretchers. Turn the quilted part under the nearside rail and open out the fabric once or twice on the far-side rail. Continue quilting until you have finished the cushion, then take the quilting out of the frame.

51

The back and front of the completed cushion.

Step 5: to finish the cushion

At this stage I must mention that I assemble all my quilting by hand, even putting on the piping, but this is a matter of personal choice. Cut along the chalk-marked line in the centre of the quilting and place the two pieces together with the wrong sides *inside* and the right sides *outside*. This is to allow the piping cord to be sewn in place. Pin the four corners together, through all the layers of the back and front, about 4in (10cm) from the points, as space must be left for the piping, see Fig 1.

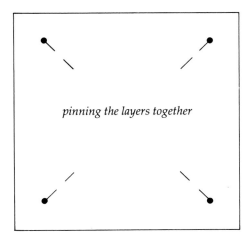

pinning the layers together

fig 1

Cut a piece of material 22in (56cm) long by 3in (7.5cm) wide for the placket facing on the front of the cushion. The short ends of the facing will be sewn into the side seams with the edges of the cushion. Sew the facing to the lining *only* of the front, with the wrong side of the facing towards the lining, leaving both raw edges at the top. These raw edges will be covered up when the piping is attached. Turn the bottom edge of the facing under for ¼in (6mm) and pin to the lining only of the front, then stitch in place. Remove the pins, see Fig 2.

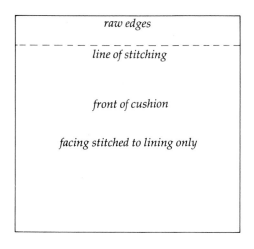

raw edges

line of stitching

front of cushion

facing stitched to lining only

fig 2

For the diamond patterned back of the cushion, cut a piece of material 18in (46cm) long by 6in (15cm) wide. This is for the placket opening of the cushion, to enable a cushion pad to be inserted. Place the right side of the placket to the right side of the top of the back and centre this, leaving about 2in (5cm) at each end and having 18in (46cm) in the centre for the opening. Pin in place. Now stitch through all the layers of the fabric.

A sample showing the placket stitched in place on the front of the cushion.

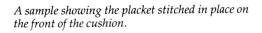

53

On the other long edge of the placket turn under a hem of about ¼in (6mm), fold the placket in half and stitch in place over the first row of stitches, covering the raw edges. Oversew both short ends, see Fig 3. Turn the placket to the inside of the opening and pin it down, so that it does not get in the way of the piping when it is being sewn in place.

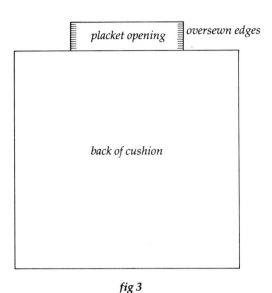

fig 3

Now take the lining *only* of the front, leaving the wadding and top material free, and all three layers of the back, and tack round the remaining three sides of the cushion and either side of the placket opening, about ¼in (6mm) in from the edge. The remaining opening is for the placket, see Fig 4.

When the front and back are tacked in this way, you are ready to begin the piping.

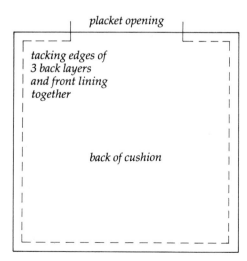

fig 4

Step 6: to make a bias piping sleeve

Cut an oblong of matching, or contrasting material, about 14in (36cm) long by 10in (25.5cm) wide. This must *not* be a square, see Fig 1. This will make approximately 50in (127cm) of bias strip for your piping cord.

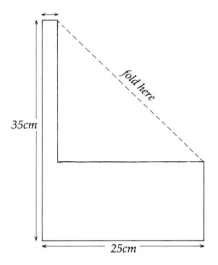

fig 1 *making a bias piping sleeve*

Take the top right-hand corner of this piece and cross over towards the left-hand corner, leaving about 1in (2.5cm) clear down the left-hand edge, see Fig 1. Cut off the folded edge, see Fig 2. Cut a 1¾in (4.5cm) wide strip of fabric from the top left-hand corner downwards, following the cut edge for 5½in (14cm). This cut is your guideline for cutting the rest of the bias strip when you have made your sleeve.

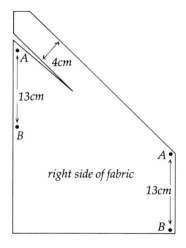

fig 2 *making the first cut*

With the right sides of the material inside, match the two points marked A together and the two points marked B. Pin the seam from A to B, ½in (1cm) in from the edge and secure with back stitch, see Fig 3.

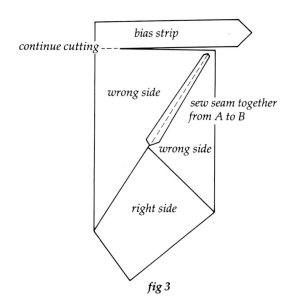

fig 3

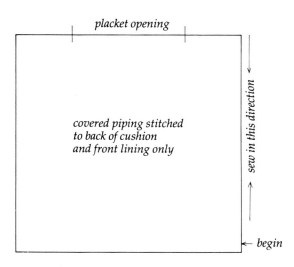

fig 1 *inserting the piping cord*

All you have to do now is begin to cut. Using the 5½in (14cm) cut you have already made as your guideline, cut round and round the fabric, straight through the back stitched seams keeping the bias strip the same width as your cut, see Fig 4. The sleeve is on the cross and in one length. this method is very useful, as it saves sewing all the bias pieces together and you can get a great deal out of a little piece of material.

Cover as much piping cord as will go all round the edges of the cushion, making piping sleeve as required, and place the cord in the centre of the wrong side of the sleeve. Put the two side edges of the strip together and tack in place but not too near the cord, as it must be left loose and not held too firmly by the sleeve. Sew together with back stitch.

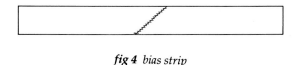

fig 4 *bias strip*

Inserting the piping cord

With the placket at the top, begin the piping at the bottom of the right-hand edge of the back, about 2in (5cm) away from the corner, see Fig 1. Take the three layers of the cushion back and the lining *only* of the front leaving the top piece of material free as this is needed later for slip stitching over the piping cord. Some of the wadding of the front will also be trimmed away later.

Place the prepared piping cord on the right side of the back, with the raw edges towards the outside edge and tack in place through all the layers, easing gently round the corners. When you come to the placket opening, continue piping along the edge but transfer the cord to the placket facing and lining only of the front and tack along the raw edges of the front,

leaving the wadding and top material free. At the end of the opening, transfer the cord to the right side of the back again and continue tacking it in place until you reach the point where you began. Stitch the piping in place. Cut the cord and join it evenly to the end already sewn on by stitching across from one to the other, making sure the ends are secure. Press into a round to match the rest of the piping.

With the right side of the cushion front facing you, begin slip stitching the top material in place to hide the edges of the piping sleeve. Make a small stitch in the folded under edge of the top material and take a very small stitch from the stitches on the piping cord edge. After each stitch, give a little pull of the cord and stitch again. The smaller the stitches the firmer the piping will be, see Fig 2.

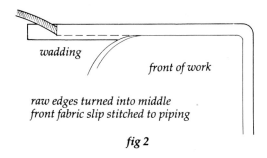

fig 2

All that is needed now are three buttons and matching buttonholes to close the placket. Linen buttons are best for quilting as they do not cut or damage the work. Sew them, evenly spaced, on the front side of the placket and make three buttonholes on the back side, stitching neatly round each buttonhole with backstitch to strengthen them and making sure they are long enough to allow the button to go through. Using about four strands of the thread used for quilting, work in buttonhole stitch round each buttonhole. Insert the cushion pad.

The old method of quilting

For those who may be interested in how things were done in the old days, or who may prefer to use this method of making a cushion, I must warn you that it requires more pre-planning at the design stage, plus a very steady hand and good eye!

Cut the material, wadding and lining and decide on the design as for the new method, then mark along the centre of the cushion.

Lay the lining on something flat and keep it firmly in place as given for transferring the design in the new method. Instead of using a paper pattern for the back of the cushion, use a chinagraph pencil and ruler to mark the diamond pattern directly on to the material, drawing lines crossways from corner to corner in both directions.

On the front of the cushion, mark the exact centre of the fabric firmly with a pencil dot. Draw a line directly on to the material all round the edges, about 1in (2.5cm) in for the piping cord. Now decide on the templates, borders and infill patterns you are going to use. If you decide on a rose motif in the centre, place the template centrally over the dot in the middle and draw directly on to the material all round it, lift off the template and complete the design freehand, copying the template. If you do not want a central motif, use the dot in the middle to position the templates exactly. If you are going to use, say, a cable border, place the template on each corner first and mark it, then try to manoeuvre the cable to fit neatly from corner to corner all round. When you are satisfied with your design, fill in with diamonds between the patterns as in the new method, making sure that no areas remain unquilted.

Put the lining, wadding and top material into the frame and begin quilting as for the new method. Take the work out of the frame and assemble the cushion as for the new method.

Personally, I find it much easier to draw the design on to the fabric in this way, rather than drawing it all out first on greaseproof paper. It means I can begin quilting that much sooner!

The finished designs

Hints for beginners

To allow for shrinkage and to ensure colour fastness, it is best to prepare cotton fabric by first washing it in hand-hot clear water. Roll in a towel smoothing out the creases, then iron whilst still very damp to restore it to its original pristine condition. This is not necessary with other fibres.

You can purchase reels of fine polyester and cotton tacking thread, which works out much less expensive than quilting thread. Try and obtain this in the same colour as the fabric as it makes finishing off easier. When the tacking thread is pulled out, some small pieces may be left behind but will not be so obvious as if they were in a contrasting colour.

The simplest way to enlarge or reduce the patterns given in this book, see page 88, is to use a pantograph. You can either make this yourself or obtain it from most art or craft shops, see Fig 1. This device consists of four flattened rods, or pieces of wood. At the appropriate points, a tracing point is fixed to one section of these rods for tracing over the lines of the original, and a drawing point to an adjacent section for making the copy. The pantograph is hinged at the crossing points and can be adjusted to enlarge or reduce the copy.

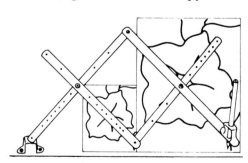

fig 1 illustration of a pantograph

You can also use a photocopier, although if you enlarge or reduce too much, the motif may not be exactly true.

For tracing round templates or over the patterns featured in this book, see page 88, you can use ordinary kitchen greaseproof paper. If you want something stronger than this, white detail (tracing) paper is available in most art shops.

When using pins in the quilting, always keep checking to make sure that these are not cutting into the material, as a tear or split cannot be repaired, no matter how to try!

You may prefer to use safety pins to secure the fabric to the tape on the side edges, but do make sure that your thread doesn't catch round the pins when quilting.

To make a full-sized bed quilt, you first need to join the fabric by hand or machine, before you can begin to quilt. The quilts given in this section take 12½yd (11.50m) of 48in (122cm) wide matching fabric for the top, the lining and the piping. Cut this material into four 3yd (2.75m) lengths, two for the lining and two for the top, leaving the rest for the piping.

Take one of these pieces and fold it lengthways, then cut it in two, making five lengths. Pin one of these cut pieces to each side of a full width, making sure the sheen of the fabric matches. Join these two seams, noting that this section is for the top of the quilt. Now take the remaining two full widths and seam them together for the lining, see Fig 2. This is so

fig 2 cutting the material for a full-sized quilt

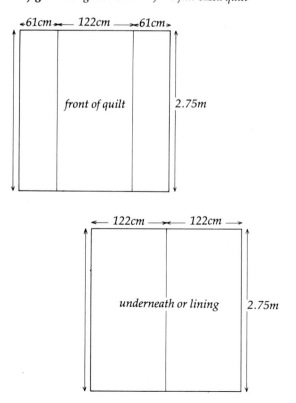

Opposite:
A wall hanging which I recently completed for a lady in Hong Kong.

58

that when the fabric is quilted, the seams are not placed together, causing extra thicknesses of material in one area which would be difficult to stitch.

To add a boxed edge and gathered frill to a fitted bed cover, first measure the exact size of the centre of the bed before beginning to quilt. Cut the fabric to this size, allowing about an extra 4in (10cm) all round to be taken up in quilting, seaming and piping. For the gathered frill and fitted box edge for the quilt shown on page 61, allow an additional amount of matching fabric sufficient to go round the two side and lower edges plus about half as much again, and to reach from the edge of the centre of the quilted section to the floor. As a rough guide you will need about 10½yd (9.50m) by 24in (61cm) deep, i.e. 5¼yd (4.75m) of 48in (122cm) wide material, cut in half lengthways.

For the beginner, the easiest modern method of transferring the design on to a pale shade of cotton is to use a water-erasable pen. However, you should never apply heat of any kind to the material once you have marked out the pattern, or the lines may become permanent.

Always remove the pattern lines when all the quilting has been completed with clean, cold water. To avoid wetting the fabric too much, apply the water with a fine plant spray, kept especially for the purpose! If you plan to use a dark-coloured fabric, mark the design with a white chinagraph pencil, which will mostly wear off as you quilt. Any remaining residue will disappear at the first washing.

For a small quilted item, an alternative method would be to set your unthreaded sewing machine to a large stitch and carefully machine round the lines in your paper pattern, making holes all the way round. Tape the paper pattern to a well-lit window, or to a glass table top with a lamp placed underneath, then tape the fabric over the paper, right side facing you. You will be able to see little pinpricks of light shining through the fabric and you can just join these up with a marker.

Some people find it easier to treat the cotton thread used for quilting cotton fabric with purified beeswax before beginning to quilt, but this is a matter of personal choice. However, this does strengthen the thread and stops it from knotting.

To wax the thread take the correct length of cotton, about 18in (46cm), and lay it across the block of beeswax. Pull it across and down into the block, so that it makes a cut in the block, to ensure that the thread is evenly coated. The wax does not mark cotton or man-made fabrics but should not be used on silk or satin.

Quilting is worked as a running stitch, which can be executed as a group of stitches, or one stitch at a time. It is obviously quicker to work groups of stitches in a

rocking movement but beginners may find this difficult. To work a stitch at a time use a separate movement downwards and then upwards through all three layers of the material. Make sure you take up the lining when working each stitch.

Whichever method you use, the stitches must be kept to the same size and this will, to some extent, be governed by the thickness of the fabric and the wadding. The aim is 10 to 12 small stitches to 1in (2.5cm) but as a beginner you will find this very hard to achieve.

Some experienced quilters like to quilt small items in the hand and do not use either a hoop or frame. This is *not* recommended for a beginner, however, as it is difficult to keep the three layers at an even tension.

As you progress in expertise you may like to experiment with this method. To avoid creasing the quilting, simply roll the work towards the centre from whichever side is convenient to the section being worked.

When working on a frame only about 18in (46cm) of the design should be visible at a time, as the hands must be able to reach all the areas without stretching.

To work a whole area of infill pattern, which does not contain any motifs, begin at the lower right-hand side of the design and work across the frame. It is easier to begin stitching motifs in the centre of the work, however, and work towards the outer areas. The quilting tends to stretch the wadding and by working from the centre, you can gradually ease out any fullness to the edges.

When the design continues beyond the visible edge, leave the needle and thread in position until the quilting is ready to be turned on the frame, so that you are ready to complete this section without any joins in the thread.

If the fabrics are washable, the best way to keep your completed quilting in good condition is to wash it by hand, in cold water with a cold-water detergent.

In the case of a full-sized bed quilt, choose a sunny day and wash it in the bath, then hang it over the line, or a rotary drier, which has first been covered with a clean sheet. Reposition the quilt frequently. When it is partially dry, lay the sheet out flat on the lawn with the quilt on top. Never iron the quilting as this will flatten the wadding.

Opposite: *a detail taken from a full sized quilt which has a boxed and frilled edge, see inset which was made from a different blue material*

Handkerchief sachet
NEW METHOD

This delightful sachet is perfect for the beginner to practice quilting and would make the ideal gift. It is made from cotton with a satin finish and the quilting has been worked in a slightly darker shade of the same colour.

The finished size is about 11in (28cm) long by 5½in (14cm) deep, when bound and folded, but these measurements do not need to be exact. It features a feather motif on the front flap, with a simple infill pattern of diagonal lines, and can be assembled by machine, or by hand if you prefer.

Materials

Two rectangles of matching fabric about 16in (40cm) long by 12in (30.5cm) wide
12in (30.5cm) square of matching fabric for bias edging
Piece of thin wadding about 16in (40cm) long by 12in (30.5cm) wide
No 7 crewel needle for tacking
No 8 between needle for quilting
Tacking thread
Quilting thread
Dressmakers' pins
Safety pins, if using frame
Thimbles or finger protectors
Purified beeswax for cotton thread, optional
Tape for frame, optional

Notes

Make a paper pattern for the sachet 11in (28cm) wide by 15in (38cm) long, rounding the corners at one end as shown in Fig 1. Mark this actual size on one of the prepared rectangles of fabric and use this for the top layer. You will then have an exact cutting line when the quilting is completed.

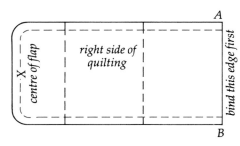

fig 1 paper pattern for handkerchief sachet

Method of designing

Choose your quilting design, either from a template or by tracing one of the designs given on page 88. Take a piece of greaseproof paper or white detail paper the same size as the paper pattern, and mark the centre of the rounded flap end on this. With a pencil position the central motif on the marked spot. Mark in the diagonal infill lines, keeping them about ½in (1cm) apart. Trace the patterns on to the top layer of the fabric.

Method of quilting

Prepare the quilting by placing the unmarked rectangle of fabric on a flat surface as the lining, wrong side up. Place the wadding on top of this then place the marked rectangle on top of this, right side up.

Tack the three layers together in a grid of about 2 to 2½in (5 to 6.5cm), see Fig 2. It is easiest to put in lines 1 to 4 first, starting at the centre each time with a loose backstitch, not a knot. Tack the other lines from side to side in alternate directions, as indicated by the arrows.

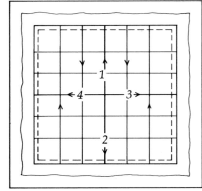

fig 2 tacking 3 layers together

Either place the prepared quilting into a hoop, or tape the side edges to the stretchers of a frame.

Commence the quilting in the centre of the motif and work outwards towards the edges. Stitch in the diagonal infill lines.

When the quilting is completed, carefully remove all the tacking. Trim away any excess lining and wadding, so that all three layers are even. Remove any remaining marker lines with clean, cold water.

The completed sachet, designed by Ann Edwards.

Leave on a flat surface away from all heat to dry naturally.

Finally, cut round the outer lines of the paper pattern shape.

Method of making up

From the 12in (30.5cm) square of fabric cut one straight strip 1½in (4cm) wide by 12in (30.5cm) long for the short straight edge of the sachet.

Pick up the bottom right-hand corner of the remaining piece of fabric and take it across to meet the top left-hand edge. Cut along this fold to give the true bias of the fabric. Cut bias strips 1½in (4cm) wide and join the pieces together to form one long strip, making straight seams, see Fig 3.

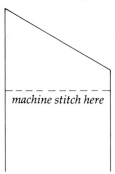

machine stitch here

fig 3 *joining bias strips*

Using the straight piece of fabric, bind the short straight edge of the sachet. Place the strip right side down on to the right side of the work and machine in place, making a ¼in (6mm) seam. Turn the strip over to the wrong side and hem down to conceal the machine stitching. Do not neaten the side edges as these will be concealed by the bias strip.

Fold up the bottom of the sachet to about one-third of its length, as indicated by the dotted line in Fig 1. Pin or tack side edges in place, with right sides facing you.

Take bias strip and with right side of sachet at the point which has been folded up and wrong side of bias facing you, begin to bind the edges at point marked A. Turn in the end of the binding and place this fold level with the bottom of the sachet. Pin or tack the binding in place all round the sachet, ending at point marked B, folding in the end of the binding as at the beginning. Machine in place all round, making a ¼in (6mm) seam. Turn binding to other side and hem in place to conceal machine stitching, trimming small amounts from seams at rounded end if necessary. Fold flap down.

Cushion with quilted front
NEW METHOD

This square cushion is suitable for the complete beginner as only the front is quilted and it is assembled by machine. The back has a simple, fold-over envelope opening, so does not need a placket or zip fastener set in.

The central design is a double feathered circle, sometimes known as a 'crown', with a feather frame and 1in (2.5cm) diamond infill. The edges are piped and a matching thread has been used for the diamonds, with a darker shade for the motif and border.

Materials

18in (46cm) long by 45in (115cm) wide cotton fabric for the top and envelope back
18in (46cm) long by 22in (56cm) wide matching fabric for the bias piping
20 × 20in (51 × 51cm) bonded 2oz (57gm) wadding
20 × 20in (51 × 51cm) cotton lining
No 7 crewel needle for tacking
No 8 between needle for quilting
Tacking thread
Quilting thread
Matching thread for machine use
Dressmakers' pins and safety pins (for frame)
2½yd (2.30m) medium piping cord
16 × 16in (40 × 40cm) square cushion pad
Thimbles or finger protectors
Zipper foot for machine
Tape for frame, optional

Notes

Lay the fabric for the top and envelope back on a flat surface. Pick up the bottom right-hand corner and take this across the fabric to meet the top edge at point marked B, see Fig 1. Cut the fabric along the dotted line, indicated by A and B. Open out this triangle and you will have a square of about 18in (46cm) for the quilted top of the cushion. The remaining piece is for the cushion back.

Take the remaining piece of cotton fabric and fold in half as indicated by the dotted line, see Fig 2. Cut along this fold. You now have two rectangles about 18in (46cm) wide by 13in (33cm) deep for the envelope back of the cushion.

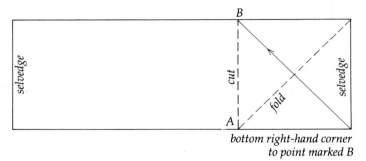

bottom right-hand corner to point marked B

fig 1 *cutting the fabric for the front*

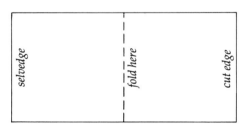

fig 2 *cutting the fabric for the back*

Method of designing

Choose your quilting design. The pattern must be marked on the right side of the 18in (46cm) top square, having first established the centre by folding the fabric lengthways then widthways and making a mark between your finger and thumb at this point.
Prepare the design by taking an 18in (46cm) square of white detail paper and mark the centre of this. Position the central motif on the marked spot, with a 2B pencil, using either a template or by tracing one of the designs given on page 88. Place the border in the same way but remember not to have this too close to the edges of the square. You should leave about 1½in (4cm) from the outer edges to ensure that none of the border is finally sewn into the ½in (1cm) seam.

Make sure the pencil lines on the paper are dark enough to enable you to trace the pattern on to the fabric, using a water erasable marker.

Above: *the quilted front of the cushion, designed by Ann Edwards.*

Right: *showing how the back of the cushion overlaps.*

Method of quilting

Prepare the quilting by placing the 20in (51cm) square of lining on a flat surface, wrong side up, place the wadding on top of this, then place the marked 18in (46cm) square on top, right side up, see Fig 3. Pin together from the centre out, keeping all three layers smooth. Now tack the three layers together in a grid of about 2 to 2½in (5 to 6.5cm) as given for the handkerchief sachet, see Fig 2. Tape the side edges to the stretchers of a frame.

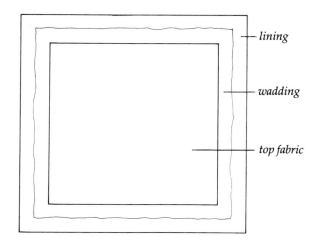

fig 3 preparing the 3 layers

Commence the quilting in the centre of the design and work outwards towards the edges.

When the quilting is completed, carefully remove all the tacking. Trim away any excess lining and wadding, so that all three layers are even. Remove any remaining marker lines with clean, cold water. Leave on a flat surface away from all heat to dry naturally.

Method of making up

Prepare the envelope back of the cushion by machining a ½in (1cm) double hem along one long side of each of the rectangles. Place to one side.

Make a bias piping strip from the matching fabric, (which will be sufficient for two cushions), by folding the fabric as shown in Fig 1. There will be a small piece on the left-hand edge to be trimmed away. Cut the square across the diagonal, making two triangles. For one cushion, take one of these triangles and cut into bias strips 1½in (4cm) wide, see Fig 4. Join pieces together to form one long strip, machining straight seams, see Fig 5.

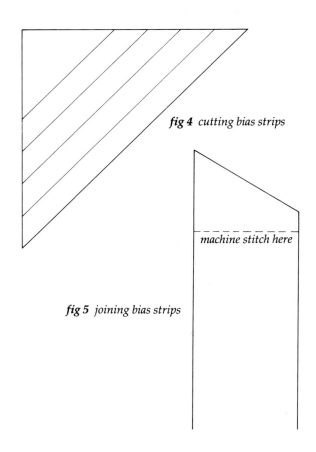

fig 4 cutting bias strips

fig 5 joining bias strips

Make the corded piping by taking the bias strip, straighten one end and turn this in for about 1¼in (3cm), see Fig 6. Place the cord in the centre, fold bias strip over with raw edges together and using a zipper foot on the machine and matching thread, begin about 1in (2.5cm) away from the folded end, see Fig 7. Continue until sufficient cord to go round all four edges of the cushion has been covered.

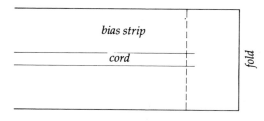

fig 6 making the piping cord

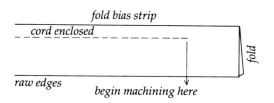

fig 7 machining the piping cord

Attach the piping cord to the top of the cushion by taking the quilted side, right side facing you, and begin in the centre of one side edge. Place the piping down on the right side of the cushion top with the raw edges together and the piping facing in towards the centre of the work. Pin, or tack in place, making three or four small nicks in the bias strip (not right up to the stitching though), at each corner to allow the piping to be eased in place. The piping will not be right at the edge of the work when rounding the corners. Continue until you come back to the starting point, adjust the length of the cord so that it will fit exactly into the folded part of the bias strip and butt right up against the beginning of the cord.

With the right side of the work facing you, machine the piping into place, sewing exactly on top of the line of stitches created when making the piping. This is very important for a firm fitting piping.

To attach the envelope back of the cushion, have the top with the piping attached with the right side facing you. Place the two rectangles, right sides down and hemmed edges overlapping each other in the centre by about 4 to 5in (10 to 13cm), over the top. These rectangles will overhang the quilted square on the outside edges by about ½in (1cm), because the quilting will have taken up some of the original measurements. Pin, or tack together.

Turn the cushion cover over, so that the wrong side of the top is now facing you. There will be a line of machine stitching created when the piping was attached to the front. Again, machine directly on to this line of stitches all the way round.

Remove the pins, or tacking, trim seams as necessary and turn right side out through the envelope opening. Insert the cushion pad.

Round boxed cushion
OLD METHOD

This luxurious cushion is worked in satin and is piped and boxed. You can have the same design on the back and front, or vary the patterns.

The completed cushion has a diameter of about 20in (51cm).

Materials

Frame, 36in (91cm) from stretcher to stretcher
40in (101.5cm) of 48in (122cm) wide fabric for both sides of cushion, boxed section and piping
40in (101.5cm) of 48in (122cm) wide fine lining material
40in (101.5cm) of 48in (122cm) bonded 2oz (57gm) wadding
Needles for tacking
Packet No 8 between needles for quilting
Tacking thread
Quilting thread
Dressmakers' pins and safety pins for frame
3½yd to 3¾yd (3 to 3.50m) medium piping cord
Round boxed cushion pad to fit
White chinagraph pencil
Thimbles or finger protectors
Tape for frame

Notes

From the top material cut a piece 22in (56cm) wide by 44in (112cm) long. Leave the remaining fabric for the boxed side section and piping. Mark across the centre with a chalk line or tacking stitch, to give two 22in (56cm) squares. Cut the lining fabric to the same size.

From thin cardboard, make a round template for the shape of the cushion, by drawing a 20in (51cm) diameter circle. Fold the card in half, then into quarters to find the centre.

Place this template on the top material, which is right side up, leaving 1in (2.5cm) round the edge for putting on the piping. Draw a line all round the template for one side of the cushion. Lift off the template. Mark the centre of the fabric with chalk. Draw another circle about ¾in (2cm) inside the first one, then another circle about ½in (1cm) inside the second, making three in all.

For the second side, place the template on the right side of the remaining top material, leaving a gap of about 2in (5cm) between the two circles. Draw a line all round the template and mark the centre. Draw two more circles as given for the first side.

Cut a strip of about 66in (168cm) long by 4in (10cm) wide for the boxed section which joins the two circles together. Draw a line ½in (1cm) in on each long edge, leaving a width of 3in (7.5cm).

From the remaining material make sufficient piping cord to go round the edges of both circles, about 126 to 132in (320 to 335cm).

Method of designing

Choose your quilting design, selecting a template such as a rose for the centre motif and place this in the centre of the first circle. Draw a line with the chinagraph pencil all round this motif and fill in freehand. Now mark in a border, such as a cable pattern, all round the edge near the third circle.

The next step is to fill in all the remaining material with an infill pattern, such as diamonds. To position the diamonds, take a 1in (2.5cm) ruler and place it on the cross of the material. Mark along each side of the ruler from the edge of the border to the centre motif, then from the other side of the centre motif to the opposite side of the border. Continue marking lines on each side of the ruler in this way until all the plain areas are filled in.

Begin again on the opposite side and rule lines which cross the first lines to form 1in (2.5cm) squares, or diamond shapes. One side of the cushion is now ready for quilting.

For the second side of the cushion either repeat the design used for the first side, select alternative patterns, fill in with diamond pattern, or use an overall pattern such as wine glass filling. To position the wine glass pattern, begin in the exact centre of the fabric and mark circles the size of the top of a wine glass, or a small teacup, across to each edge. Mark another row of circles in the same way above and below the first line, then continue until all the plain areas are filled in. Now position and mark another set of circles over the first ones, see wine glass pattern page 89.

For the boxed section, fill in the whole area with small diamonds, making sure they are positioned on the cross of the material.

Method of framing

Place two small tables in position and rest the frame on top. Take the lining material and pin this to the webbing on both rails, see page 45 for preparing the frame.

After both edges are sewn into the frame, take the far side and wind it round the rail, with the wrong side of the fabric facing you. Put in the stretchers and place the pegs in position, gently pulling the lining to make sure it is not too taught, as it must be picked up when stitching through the three layers.

Now place the wadding on top of the lining and the marked material on top of this with the design facing you. Tack along the front edge through the three layers of material, leaving any surplus wadding and the remainder of the cushion top hanging over the fair rail of the frame.

At the far side rail see that the wadding is straight and pull the top material over the wadding. Use pins to catch through all three layers every 2 to 3in (5 to 7.5cm) apart. Do not have it too tight as you must be able to pick up the lining with the stitches.

Now tape the work into the frame by pinning the tape through all three layers, see page 45 for preparing the frame. Keep away from the pattern areas.

Method of quilting

Prepare the needles and begin quilting by joining in with a knot, see page 50 beginning to quilt. Quilt from front to back and from right to left, unless you are left-handed, in which case work from left to right.

It is best to quilt about half of one of the marked circles before turning the work on. Continue until the quilting on both circles is completed. Take out of the frame. Cut round the circles about 1in (2.5cm) from the outside edge.

Put the lining for the boxed section into the frame, then the wadding and the marked fabric, with the design facing you. Quilt all the diamonds and remove from the frame.

Method of making up

Sew the piping cord to the outside chalk line of both circles with back stitch. When you have completed the piping and are back where you began, take the end of the cord up to the beginning and join these together, stitching across from one end to the other and making sure they are secure. Cover the join by wrapping the surplus material from the end of the piping sleeve over it, then slip stitch in place. Cut off any surplus wadding and lining.

To join the boxed section to the top and bottom circles, pin the edge of the strip round the edge of one circle, placing the right sides together with the piping sleeve between them and pointing towards the centre. Back stitch firmly all round the cushion, removing the pins as you go.

Join the other edge of the strip to the other circle, leaving an opening of about 15in (38cm) for the placket.

Cut off any surplus material from the strip and join the two short ends together with back stitch. Back stitch firmly all round the cushion, removing the pins as you go.

At the placket opening, sew a piece of material 15in (38cm) long by 2in (5cm) wide to the piping of the top side of the cushion with back stitch. Turn it underneath and slip stitch along on the wrong side, so that the piping is between the cut pieces. On the box section pin, then back stitch another strip of material 15in (38cm) long by 4in (10cm) wide in place, with the right sides facing each other. Turn the material to the inside of the boxed edge and hem down on the wrong side.

The cushion is now complete. Turn to the right side. Insert the cushion pad and lightly slip stitch the placket edge to the piping edge.

This luxurious round cushion is boxed and piped.

Full-sized quilt
OLD METHOD

The experienced quilter will now long to begin a full-sized bed cover. Two methods are given for making the gold quilt shown opposite, one using the old method of quilting and the other the new method, see pages 43 to 56 for details of the techniques.

The completed quilt measures about 94in (239cm) wide by 106in (269cm) long.

Materials

Frame, 3yd (2.75m) long from stretcher to stretcher
12½yd (11.50m) of 48in (122cm) wide matching fabric for the top, lining and piping
3 lengths of 96in (244cm) by 40in (101.5cm) wide bonded 2oz (57gm) wadding
Needles for tacking
Packet No 8 between needles for quilting
Tacking thread
Quilting thread
Dressmakers' pins and safety pins for frame
11½yd (10.50m) medium piping cord
White chinagraph pencil
Thimbles or finger protectors
Tape for frame

Notes

Cut and seam the fabric as given in hints for beginners, see page 58.

From the remaining fabric, make a piping sleeve about 11½yd (10.50m) long, or sufficient to go round all four edges of the quilt.

Method of designing

Choose your quilt design, selecting a template such as a rose for the centre motif and, say, a feather pattern round this. Always fill as much of the centre as you can with suitable motifs, not leaving too much infill pattern, such as diamonds. The craft of quilting is centred on the designs, and this stage is an art in itself and should not be rushed. Find the centre of the top section of the quilt by folding the fabric lengthways, then widthways, and mark this point with a chalk pencil which will rub off in quilting.

Place a large leather or plastic table mat on a suitable table top and lay the top section of material over this,

right side up and making sure it is straight. Take a ruler and chinagraph pencil and draw all round the edges, about 1in (2.5cm) in from the edge. Now draw another line about ½in (1cm) inside the first line. This looks like a picture frame and is used when fitting the piping cord.

Begin drawing in the design, filling in the central motif and borders first. Place the corner template, such as a cable pattern, in each corner, draw round it and fill in freehand from the template. To fill the corner motif up a bit, place a motif such as a small rose inside it.

Continue until you are satisfied with the design, making sure that each motif is correctly placed and that the patterns are all filled in by freehand.

The next step is to fill in all the remaining areas with an infill pattern, such as the diamonds used here. To position the diamonds, take a 1in (2.5cm) wide ruler, or long piece of wood, place it at the right-hand corner of the design pointing towards the centre. Begin marking at each side of the ruler. Lift the ruler and make a second mark, then continue marking all the lines on each side of the ruler until all the plain areas are filled in, from corner to corner. Turn the quilt round and begin marking the lines from corner to corner again, in the opposite direction. The diamonds should be 1in (2.5cm) squares, not lozenge shapes. Diamond patterns are quilted on the cross of the material, which gives a nice wavy stitch.

Be sure to take the infill pattern right up to the motifs, remembering that no spaces over 2in (5cm) should be left.

Method of framing

Place two tables, or trestles in position and rest the frame on top. Take the lining material and pin this to the webbing on both rails, see page 45 for preparing the frame.

After both edges are sewn into the frame, take the farthest side and wind it round and round the rail,

Opposite: instructions are given for making this gold quilt by either the old or the new method of quilting, see inset. The background shows a close-up detail of the design.

with the wrong side of the material facing you. Turn until there is about 20in (51cm) left, put in the stretchers and place one peg in each end, pull gently then place in the third peg and at the other end place in the fourth peg. Test again to see that the lining is not too taut, as it must be picked up when stitching through the three layers.

Now place the wadding in position. Begin at the right-hand stretcher and roll one piece lengthways across to the opposite stretcher. Make sure it is nice and smooth with no lumpy or thin areas. Join sections of wadding together when required, see page 41.

With the design on the top material facing you, place this on top of the wadding, leaving the surplus wadding and the rest of the top of the quilt hanging over the far rail of the frame.

On the near side rail, which is the front of the frame, pin through all three layers of material from stretcher to stretcher. Then tack through all the layers, removing the pins as you come to them. On the far side rail, or back edge, see that the wadding is straight and pull the top material to the edge of this rail and over the wadding and lining. Pull gently to make sure the top is perfectly straight, then use pins to catch through all three layers every 2 to 3in (5 to 7.5cm) apart. This keeps the work firm and straight but remember not to have it too tight. You must be able to pick up the lining when stitching and both sides of the work must be alike.

Now tape the work into the frame by pinning the tape through all three layers, see page 45 preparing the frame, keeping away from the pattern areas. To keep the material firm and stop it becoming soiled or creased, take the wadding and quilt top which are hanging over the far side of the frame and place them into folds, then pin to the edge of the quilt near the stretcher ends.

Method of quilting

Prepare the needles and begin quilting, see page 50 beginning to quilt, joining in with a knot. Start on the two straight lines which form the frame for the piping around the edges. Take the needle slantways through all three layers and feel for the point of the needle on the forefinger of the non-working hand and use the forefinger of the working hand to help lift the stitches on to the needle. Try doing three or four stitches in this way, then draw the thread through, give a gentle tug to make the stitches take up the material and give the characteristic puffed effect of quilting. When you feel confident, try making six or more stitches at a time. Do not attempt any of the motifs until you are well into the swing of quilting, and always work from the front to the back of the frame.

When you have completed the two lines as far as you can go at arms length, begin on the first motif, then complete the whole section, including any infill patterns. Remember that when quilting diamonds you go as far as you can, then come down again, making 'tent' shapes.

When you are ready to turn the work on, remove the tapes and stretchers, fold the quilted part over the front rail, making the turn underneath so that the top fabric is uppermost. For every turn under at the front, take out the same amount at the back, ready to begin quilting again.

Replace the stretchers, then pin on the tapes where you are going to recommence quilting. Once the halfway mark is reached, you will find the rest of the work goes very quickly!

Once all the work is quilted, check that all the patterns have been filled in and that the quilt is ready to take out of the frame. Take off the tapes, then remove all the pins. Cut the quilt out of the frame by cutting along both sides of the webbing on the rails to release the lining but be very careful not to cut into the top layer of the quilt.

Trim the layers so that they are even, leaving at least 1in (2.5cm) all round the edges for the piping. As quilting takes up the top layer, as much as 2in (5cm) may need to be trimmed from the wadding and lining.

Method of making up

Commence about half-way along the bottom edge on the wrong side of the work and place the piping cord about ½in (1cm) from the edge of the lining only. Work a few back stitches to secure it, pull lightly then continue working in back stitch along the edge. The wadding and top fabric are left free and will eventually be slip stitched all round on the right side of the work. Continue in back stitch round all the edges, remembering to pull the cord regularly to give a nice straight finish to the edge. When coming to a corner, make a few extra stitches before stitching along the next edge.

When you have completed sewing in the piping and are back where you began, take the end up to the beginning of the cord and cut both ends even. Join the ends together, stitching across from one end to the other and making sure that they are secure. Cover the join by wrapping the surplus material from the end of the piping sleeve over it and back stitch in place. Make the join as straight and smooth as possible so that it matches the rest of the piping.

Turn the quilt to the right side and trim the wadding to fit neatly between the quilted stitches on the top layer and up to the raw edges of the piping cord, so that it lies flat.

Begin slip stitching the piping cord in place on the right side of the quilt, away from any corners. Lay the top material over the wadding and turn the edge under, keeping it straight. Begin with a knot and take small stitches from the ones already made on the piping cord, then a slightly larger stitch from the top edge of the quilted layer. Continue round all the edges. The slip stitches will bring the edge of the fabric up to the piping cord and will not be seen, but do keep checking that the material is straight and not gathered up or puckered.

Full-sized quilt
NEW METHOD

The main difference between the old and the new method of quilting is the way in which the design is transferred on to the material. In the old method it is marked straight on to the fabric; in the new method it is first traced out on to greaseproof or white detail paper, see pages 43 to 44 for details of the techniques.

The completed quilt measures about 94in (239cm) wide by 106in (269cm) long.

Materials

Frame, 3yd (2.75m) long from stretcher to stretcher
12½yd (11.50m) of 48in (122cm) wide matching fabric for the top, lining and piping
3 lengths of 96in (244cm) by 40in (101.5cm) wide bonded 2oz (57gm) wadding
Needles for tacking
Packet No 8 between needles for quilting
Tacking thread
Quilting thread
Dressmakers' pins and safety pins for frame
11½yd (10.50m) medium piping cord
Cobbler's awl for transferring the design
Roll of 48in (122cm) wide greaseproof paper
Tablecloth or sheeting for transferring the design
Thimbles or finger protectors
Tape for frame

Notes

Cut and seam the fabric as given in hints for beginners, see page 58.

From the remaining fabric, make a piping sleeve about 11½yd (10.50m) long, or sufficient to go round all four edges of the quilt.

Cut the greaseproof or white detail paper into four pieces 48in (122cm) wide by 54in (137cm) long. When placed together, these will cover the material for the top of the quilt.

Method of designing

Choose the motifs, border and infill patterns for your design. Fill in as much of the centre as possible with a suitable design, not leaving too much plain for an infill pattern.

Take one piece of the greaseproof paper and lay it on a firm table top. This will cover one-quarter of the quilt area. Using a ruler, with a pencil draw a line 1in (2.5cm) in from the edge on two sides of the paper. The remaining sides left plain will join with the other three pieces. Draw a second line about ½in (1cm) inside the first line. This makes a frame and is used when fitting the piping cord.

Start drawing one quarter of the design on to the greaseproof paper. Begin in the corner where the lines have already been drawn and position the chosen border pattern on these two sides, but not too close to the edges, then draw round the template.

Now mark the template selected as the round centre motif into four quarters and position the centre of one of these quarters exactly in the corner of the remaining two plain edges of the greaseproof paper. The remaining three separate quarters will be drawn on to the other pieces of paper in the same way. Draw round the template, filling in the details freehand. If this is difficult, just place the template underneath the paper to the outline already drawn and trace over the details.

When the first quarter has been completed, copy the next three sections by placing them, one at a time, over this and pencil in the rest of the design, keeping the lines firm and even. When the four pieces are

Making quilted clothing for a doll
will give you the confidence to tackle
garments for babies or adults.

butted together, you will be able to see the effect of the whole design.

Method of transferring the design

Take a large tablecloth or sheet and fold into four thicknesses, then place it evenly on to a table. Lay the quilt top material on the folded cloth, keeping it flat and straight with no creases. Pin this to the sheeting all round the edges about every 2in (5cm).

Place the greaseproof paper design on top of the fabric, with the centre design exactly in the centre of the material and, again, pin all round the edges right through the paper, quilt top and layers of sheeting. Make sure there are no creases anywhere or you may cut the material in the process of transferring the design – easily done! Also ensure that the pencil marked side of the paper is *uppermost* and not facing the fabric.

To transfer the design take a ruler and the awl and begin on the outside border lines. Place the ruler near the first line and with the awl in the working hand, press the fingers of the other hand on the ruler and with the awl held slantways, not on the point, run it along the side of the ruler lightly once or twice. Do not press it too hard, just enough to make a groove in the material, which is very plain to see when quilting.

The ruler will not be of any help when transferring the motifs. With the awl in the working hand, use the fingertips of the other hand to press down the edge of the template and press round every curve with the awl, moving the fingers all the time to keep the work in place.

Do not remove the greaseproof paper while you are transferring the design. The paper will be cut and not suitable to use again. When one quarter of the design has been marked on the fabric, complete the remaining sections one at a time, making sure the centre motif fits exactly.

Methods of framing, quilting and making up

Follow the instructions given under these headings for the quilt shown on page 70.

Making garments

You need to be a competent dressmaker and quilter to successfully complete a garment. Small items can be assembled by hand but machining gives a better finish to a large garment, such as a dressing gown.

Materials

Using a dressing gown as an example, the first thing to obtain is a suitable paper pattern. You must then calculate the total amount of material and wadding required.

If both sides of the garment are to be reversible you will need double the amount of matching fabric given in the paper pattern. As a guide, if the pattern states 4yd (3.75m) of 48in (122cm) wide material, you will require 8yd (7.50m) plus extra for the piping, say 8½yd (7.75m). You will also need wadding to the original size given in the paper pattern.

For a small garment where too much weight would be a disadvantage, such as a baby's dress, you could use a fine muslin as the quilted lining. Similarly, if a garment is completed with a separate lining, such as a jacket, it need not be reversible and you could use a fine cotton for the quilted lining. In both instances, buy the original amount of top material given in the pattern, (plus extra for the piping), and a similar amount for the quilted lining. You will also need wadding to the original amount given and, in the case of a garment with a separate lining, the original amount of material needed for this.

Notes

Again using a dressing gown as an example, lay the material lengthways on a table, then study the paper pattern and see how it will fit on to the fabric. Place the back in position first then the two fronts, one front to a selvedge edge and the other on the opposite selvedge edge. Make sure you have a right and left front, not two fronts alike as they cannot be altered once they are quilted. Position the sleeves next, noting that these must also be reversed, not two the same. Lastly, arrange the collar, belt, pockets and cuffs, if required, on the remaining material.

Take a chinagraph pencil and mark all round the pattern pieces. Use these as a guide for positioning the design and for cutting and assembling the sections once the quilting has been taken out of the frame.

Method of designing

Choose suitable motif, border and infill patterns. Commence at the bottom of the back with a border pattern, such as a cable or feather, as both stand out well. Add extra motifs to go about a third of the way up the back, then fill in with something like a diamond pattern.

Now continue the same designs used for the back on the fronts, working the border to the corner and, if required, up the front edge. An additional template could be placed in the corner, inside the border, to help fill it up.

Work the same border and patterns on the sleeves to go about three-quarters of the way up, then fill in with diamond pattern.

The design on the lower edges of the sections should join exactly at the seams. However, infill patterns, such as diamonds, will not always join up exactly, as some garments are shaped. Collar, cuffs and pocket tops always look effective when a small cable pattern is used.

When you are satisfied with the design, mark round all the templates with a chinagraph pencil and fill in freehand. Check again for any mistakes and rectify.

Methods of framing and quilting

Follow the instructions given under these headings for the quilt shown on page 70.

Method of making up

Follow any specific instructions given in the paper pattern.

This warm wrapover dressing gown is suitable for a man or a woman but you can also shorten it to make a smoking jacket for a man.

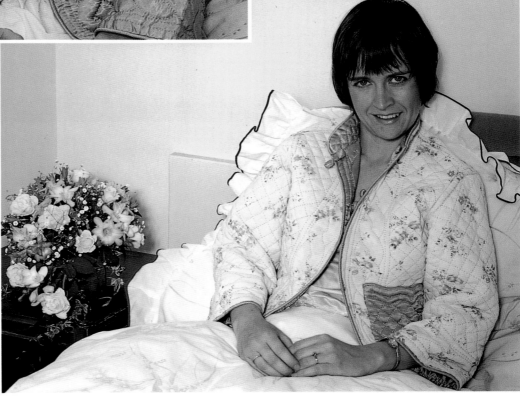

77

A complete matinee set for the new arrival.

Opposite: *this beautiful Christening dress and matching bonnet, see inset, will become a family heirloom. The background shows a close-up detail of the design.*

The three eiderdowns shown on these pages are not as closely stitched as a traditional quilt and I use them in my cottage on cold winter nights. **Opposite***: top, the centre of this eiderdown is quilted and piped; bottom, a closely-quilted edge is the feature on this example.* **Above***: here again, the centre of the eiderdown is quilted and piped.*

81

The quilt illustrated on these two pages comes from America. It is embroidered in cross stitch and then quilted afterwards.

This started out as a photograph of the quilt on my bed but we gradually added many of the other items I have scattered around my cottage!
It may provide you with some design ideas.

The top picture shows me quilting at the Quilts UK exhibition at Malvern in 1990. In the lower picture I am presenting an award to Marie-Jose Michel of France at the same exhibition.

Relaxing in my favourite armchair!

Infill and
template patterns

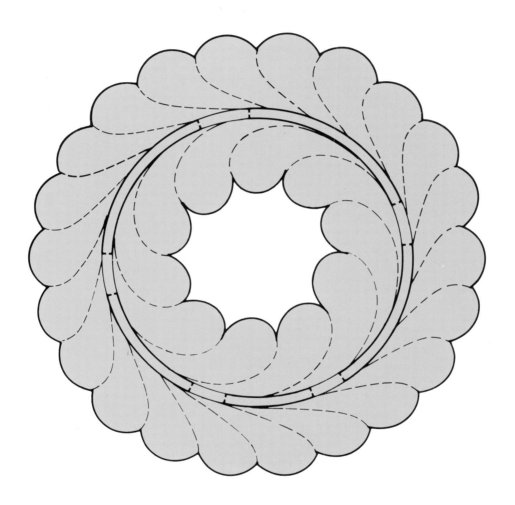

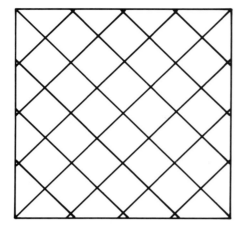

square diamond pattern

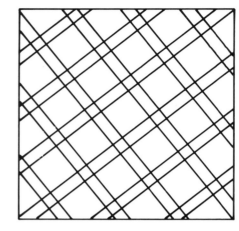

double diamond pattern

Victorian diamond pattern

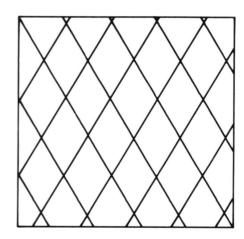

true diamond pattern

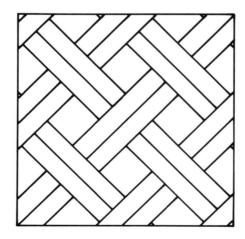

basket pattern

wave pattern

wineglass pattern

shell pattern

wave and shell pattern

star pattern

feathered circle

rose in a ring

open flower

Weardale wheel

lovers' knot

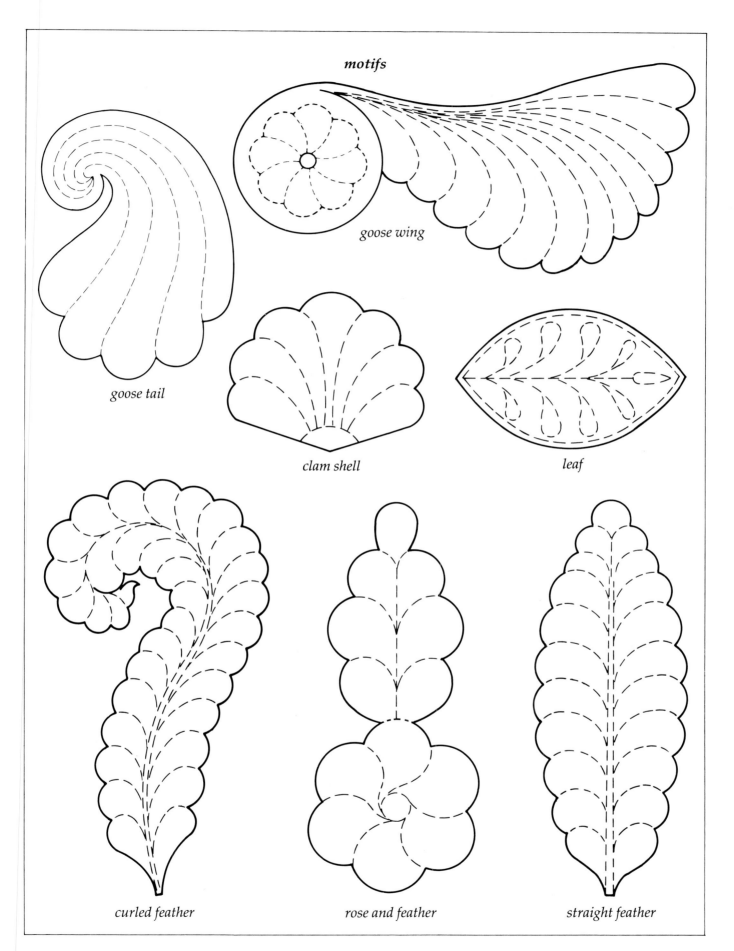

motifs

goose wing

goose tail

clam shell

leaf

curled feather

rose and feather

straight feather

91

corners and borders

penny ha'penny

wave border

trail border

cable border

line and feather border

running feather border

Weardale chain border

92

plaited border

feather twist border and corner

chain border and corner

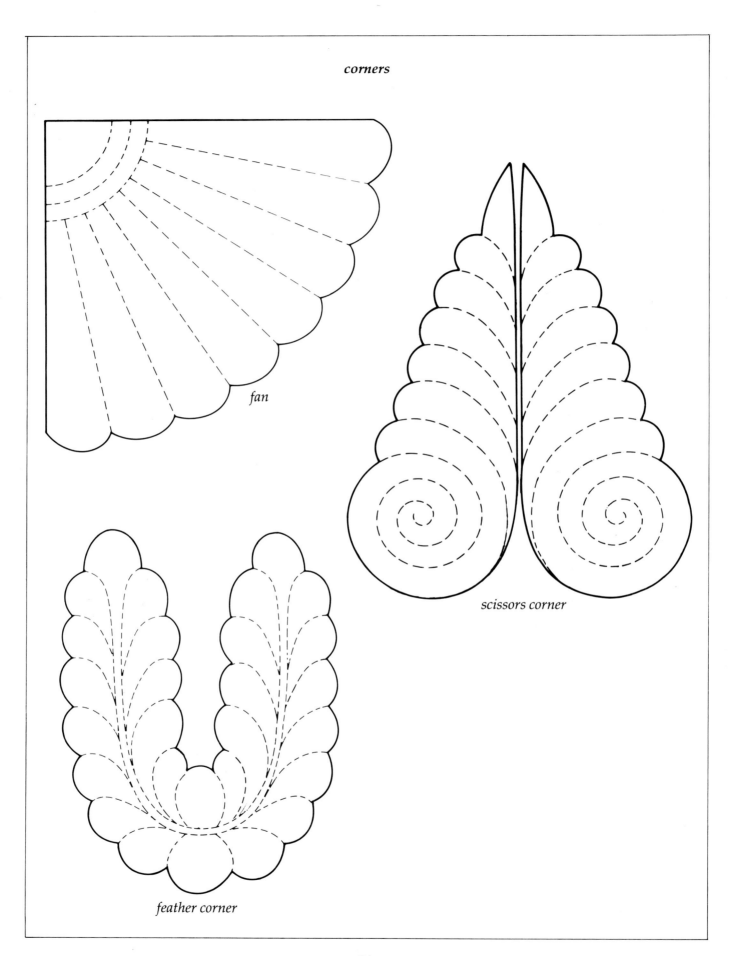

fan

scissors corner

feather corner

Index

OTHER BOOKS PUBLISHED BY SEARCH PRESS

EVERY KIND OF PATCHWORK
Edited by Kit Pyman

'Really lives up to its title and is sufficiently easy to follow that even the most helpless needleperson would be tempted to have a go.' *The Guardian*

EVERY KIND OF SMOCKING
Edited by Kit Pyman

'Filled with colour photographs, diagrams, patterns and packed with project ideas, this book will inspire readers and embroiderers to add their own contribution to the continuation of this rewarding craft.' *Workbox*

MADE TO TREASURE:
Embroideries for all Occasions
Edited by Kit Pyman

This book offers a wide variety of ideas for creating attractive embroideries to commemorate an event or occasion. 'A delightful book which can be dipped into time and time again . . .' *Workbox*

GOLD AND SILVER EMBROIDERY
Edited by Kit Pyman

'It is a comprehensive guide to gold and silver embroidery and shows how basic techniques can be used to build beautiful designs. There are ideas for everything from sequins to silk purses.' *Farmlife*

EMBROIDERED LANDSCAPES
Kit Pyman

Create your own beautiful embroidered landscapes using the simple techniques and ideas illustrated in this book. Exploring colour, texture, mood, light and shade Kit Pyman offers a colourful collection of embroideries for beginners and experienced needleworkers.

THE ART OF PAINTING ON SILK
Volume One
Edited by Pam Dawson

A full description of the basic silk painting techniques, and range of materials required, is followed by colourful examples of stunning designs and finished items. 'A useful guide for the beginner.' *Artists & Illustrators Magazine*

THE SPLENDID SOFT TOY BOOK
Erna Rath

'. . . gives an excellent and completely illustrated account of soft toy making . . . toys range from a baby's first teddy bear to the elegant and sophisticated collectors' dolls.'
Do-it-Yourself Magazine

SCANDINAVIAN CROSS STITCH
Inga Bergfeldt

Containing a delightful collection of patterns for embroidery on linen and cotton, this book offers thirty-six projects for pillows, tablecloths, table napkins, mats, sachet pillows and pincushions all of which make elegant accessories for the home.

HOW TO MAKE AND DESIGN CHURCH KNEELERS
Angela Dewar and Gisela Banbury

Many colourful examples of kneelers are illustrated together with guidance on which tools and materials are required, which stitches to use, and ideas for sources of design.

EMBROIDERED HOUSES AND GARDENS
Kit Pyman

This book will encourage any needlewoman to embroider her own home on to canvas. Instructions on the transfer of the design are given as well as suggestions for different embroidery techniques.

EMBROIDERED FLOWERS
Kit Pyman

Containing a delightful collection of flower embroideries and accompanied by full colour illustrations and simple instructions, this book gives help through all the stages from the initial idea to the finished flower embroidery.

Search Press also publishes the popular and highly successful Needlecraft series, edited by Kit Pyman, which has been specially designed to appeal to both beginners and experienced needleworkers.

If you are interested in any of the above books or any of the art and craft titles published by Search Press, please send for a free catalogue to:
Search Press Ltd., Dept B, Wellwood, North Farm Road, Tunbridge Wells, Kent TN2 3DR.